STUDENT'S
GO
VEGAN
COOKBOOK

ALSO BY CAROLE RAYMOND

Student's Vegetarian Cookbook

Over 135 Quick, Easy, Cheap, and Tasty Vegan Recipes

CAROLE RAYMOND

STUDENT'S
GO
VEGAN
COOKBOOK

Three Rivers Press / New York

Three Rivers Press and the Tugboat design are registered trademarks of
Random House, Inc.

Library of Congress Cataloging-in-Publication Data

Raymond, Carole, 1939–
Student's go vegan cookbook : over 135 quick, easy, cheap,
and tasty vegan recipes / Carole Raymond.
p. cm.
1. Vegan cookery. 2. Low-budget cookery. 3. Quick-and-easy cookery. I. Title.

TX837.R3792 2006
641.5'636—dc22
2006009252

ISBN-13: 978-0-307-33653-8
ISBN-10: 0-307-33653-0

Printed in the United States of America

Design by Elina D. Nudelman

10 9 8 7 6 5 4 3 2 1

First Edition

This book is dedicated to my

courageous and truthful mother, who taught me how to dance,

and to my stepfather,

whose life is a lesson to all of us in the art of kindness.

Acknowledgments

Thank you to my good friend Roberta Miller, for her constant patience, her preference for order, and her invaluable advice.

I am grateful to my husband, Richard Raymond, who reminded me along the way to laugh a lot.

And giant hugs and deepest thanks to my children, family, and friends.

Special thanks and appreciation to Brandi Bowles, my editor at Random House, for her enthusiastic help in making this book better in every way.

Thank you to Kathryn McHugh at Random House, for her help in the beginning of this process; and thanks to Elina Nudelman, for her design, and Rita Madrigal, for her copyediting.

Contents

Vegan Perspective

When you're cramming for a physics final and hunger pangs hit at 3 A.M., what do you do? If you're a vegan, you don't call Domino's or grab a pint of frozen yogurt from the freezer. But you can turn to the recipes in the *Student's Go Vegan Cookbook* and enter a world of great-tasting food in a matter of minutes.

Vegan students are like other students—short on time and money, hungry for variety, and sometimes in need of comfort food. Whether you're a full-time vegan enthusiast or a flexitarian who eats mostly vegetables, *Student's Go Vegan Cookbook* meets your needs with easy, inexpensive meals full of color and flavor. You'll find recipes that tantalize the most discerning palates, including Creamy Portobello Mushroom Soup (page 90), Crusty Tempeh Cutlets (page 201), Jicama and Orange Salad (page 100), Dark Chocolate Rice Pudding (page 209), One-Pot Pasta (page 167), and Pumpkin Scones (page 92). When you feel like a night of conversation, invite your friends into the kitchen and cook up a fresh, crowd-pleasing pizza.

People who enjoy a vegan diet are often quizzed with questions such as "What *do* you eat?" The answer is every food on the planet—except for animal-derived items such as meat, fish, eggs, cheese, milk, and honey. The vegan table is laden with fresh fruits and vegetables, whole grains, beans, and nuts. But figuring out how to prepare plant-based foods can seem formidable to those of us who didn't grow up learning how to cook this way. The *Student's Go Vegan Cookbook* suggests how to stock a vegan pantry and offers cooking tips and liberating recipes. Whatever your position on the food philosophy continuum, and whatever your culinary experience, the *Student's Go Vegan Cookbook* will be your partner in preparing satisfying snacks and meals any time of the day or night.

Food for Thought

Records on food history dating back as far as the fifth century B.C. find the Greek philosophers Pythagoras and Plato espousing fleshless eating. People are attracted to plant-based diets for reasons of personal and environmental health, ethics, and religion. Whatever the reason, today it's common to see shopping carts piled with tofu, soy milk, and veggie burgers.

Vegan Basics—Getting All You Need

People choosing a vegan lifestyle want to know: Is it safe? Will I get enough protein? Will I get the full range of nutrients without meat and dairy products? The answer to all three questions is a resounding yes. Researchers have verified that a balanced, whole-food vegan diet is positively good for you. Vegan eating is about thriving.

Protein

When diets contain enough calories and an assortment of plant foods over the course of a day, it's easy for people in the United States and other developed countries to get enough protein. Whole-grain breads, cereals, nuts, seeds, tofu, beans, lentils, and seitan are especially good sources. Some people mistakenly think they must eat meat in order to be strong, yet a number of the planet's biggest animals (for example, elephants, bulls, and stallions) thrive on vegan diets.

The question surrounding the amount of protein a person needs continues to be examined by researchers, and some studies are beginning to suggest that the typical American diet may include too much protein for optimal health.

Vitamin B$_{12}$

Humans require only about 2 to 3 micrograms of vitamin B$_{12}$ per day. It is an essential vitamin that your body uses for the synthesis of red blood cells and the maintenance of your nervous system.

All of the vitamin B$_{12}$ in the world ultimately comes from bacteria. Neither plants nor animals can make it. These bacteria are all over the world in the wind, soil, and water.

When animals eat particles of soil along with grass or feed, the vitamin ends up in their flesh, milk, and eggs. Nonvegans receive their vitamin B$_{12}$ from animals.

The problem for vegans is that no one knows how much B$_{12}$ may be on an unwashed apple, lettuce leaf, or carrot, and you cannot count on bottled or chlorinated water for the vitamin. The best way for vegans to get vitamin B$_{12}$ is through fortified foods such as breakfast cereals, soy or grain beverages, some meat substitutes, and supplements.

Vitamin D

Getting adequate vitamin D is necessary for the absorption of calcium. Most foods lack this vitamin, and fortified foods are the major dietary source for everyone, vegans and nonvegans alike. Make sure the soy and grain beverages you select contain added vitamin D. Our bodies manufacture a significant amount of the vitamin when our skin is exposed to sunlight, so consider talking a walk in the fresh air and getting some vitamin D at the same time.

Calcium

Calcium is an important nutrient for building strong bones, and the advertisements pushing milk as the answer are inescapable. But milk is actually only one of the many foods that supply calcium. A strong debate is going on among scientists over what are the best sources and how much calcium a person needs. Until the debate is settled, here is a list of calcium-rich foods.

Calcium-fortified orange juice
Tofu made with calcium sulfate
Calcium-fortified soy milk
Calcium-fortified rice milk
Calcium-fortified breakfast cereals, such as Special K Low
    Carb Lifestyle Protein Plus
Collard greens
Kale
Okra
Unsulfured blackstrap molasses
Broccoli
Beans
Black-eyed peas
Bok choy
Sesame seeds
Sesame tahini
Figs

Exercise

Although studying for hours burns mental energy, your body and mind need physical exercise to function at their peak.

The United States Department of Agriculture (USDA) has been doling out information about nutrition since 1916, but it's taken nearly one hundred years for the government to mention the importance of exercise. MyPyramid, the newest USDA food pyramid, includes a drawing of a man climbing stairs. The figure was added to emphasize the importance of balancing food intake with energy expenditure. The corresponding slogan, "Steps to a Healthier You," highlights the idea that small steps toward a better diet, along with exercise, can make a big difference in overall health. Harvard University made an even stronger statement in designing its new health guide by clearly making exercise the foundation of its food pyramid.

Maintaining strong muscles makes it easier to maintain a healthy weight. Muscle is an active tissue and consumes energy. It uses the calories in the food you eat. Body fat, on the other hand, has low energy requirements and uses few calories. People who don't exercise begin to lose muscle in their mid-twenties, and unless they decrease their calorie intake, they will gain weight. Engaging in regular exercise makes it possible to sustain more muscle mass and to stay fit.

Exercise doesn't just help you look trim; it is essential for overall health. It's especially important for young women in helping slow down osteoporosis later in life. Preventing osteoporosis depends on two things: making the strongest, densest bones possible during the first thirty years of life, and limiting the amount of bone loss in adulthood. Getting regular exercise with resistance training, jogging, and walking helps your bones and muscles stay strong.

Learning the Labels

You have probably noticed the increasing number of savvy shoppers clogging supermarket aisles studying the information on cans, jars, and boxes. They realize that just because a cereal package shows a picture of ripe blueberries on the front, it may not contain real fruit. And if a carton says "orange juice," it may not contain 100 percent juice. By law, however, the Nutrition Facts portion of the label cannot lie; it must list the ingredients in order of predominance. Reading the label lets you know what's in the package and what's missing.

* Finding whole-grain food may not be as easy as it appears at first glance. Food companies know consumers are interested in buying whole grains, so they make it difficult for you to know if what you're buying is diluted with refined flour. If a bread label lists fiber as 1 gram per slice, something's probably missing—specifically, the outer layer of the bran that contains the grain's natural nutrients. True whole-grain products list as the main ingredients whole wheat, whole oats, whole rye, or some other whole grain. If the label says, "made with wheat flour," it may be whole wheat or it may not be. (Even glazed sugar doughnuts are made with wheat flour.)

* Look for fortified foods. Choose breads and cereals with added vitamin B_{12}. Buy fruit juice enriched with calcium and vitamin D. Select nondairy beverages fortified with calcium and vitamin D. Look for tofu made with calcium sulfate.

* Steer clear of "bad" fats. Tropical oils (coconut, palm kernel, and palm) are highly saturated fats. You'll find them in commercial cookies, cakes, and some energy bars. Saturated fat has a negative effect on total cholesterol, so it is important to limit it in your diet. Trans fats are produced when liquid vegetable oils are hydrogenated, turning the liquid oil into a solid. Most trans fats are found in commercially prepared baked goods, snack foods, and processed foods. Check out the label on vegan and vegetarian foods, too. Soy margarine, vegan sausages, and vegan burgers may contain hydrogenated fat. There is no middle ground in the research concerning this fat. It is a health hazard and bad for your arteries. Avoid products that list trans fats on the Nutrition Facts section of the label.

* What about sweeteners? Reject products made with high-fructose corn syrup. It is a highly refined product and preliminary scientific research suggests high-fructose corn syrup (HFCS) works differently inside the body than other sugars. HFCS may trigger fat storage and can be a causative factor in heart disease. It is found in everything from pizza to soda pop, and it's in many energy bars.

Honey is a natural sweetener, but it is not a vegan ingredient because many bees are killed or harmed when honey is taken from their hives.

The use of white sugar, brown sugar, and powdered sugar in a vegan diet is a matter of personal choice. Twenty-five percent of all sugar is purified through charcoal filters made from animal bones. Bone residue does not become part of the finished product and some vegans continue to use sugar. There are alternatives to sugar and honey, such as pure maple syrup, barley malt syrup, rice syrup, molasses, agave nectar, dried cane juice granules, fruit juice, fruit juice concentrate, raisins, dates, and bananas.

* Watch out for the low-fat deception. Low-fat alternatives often have just as many calories as full-fat versions, and maybe even more. Low-fat products can be full of sugar to make up for taste when the fat is removed.

* Notice the serving sizes. Sometimes these are unrealistically small and may be eating more salt or fat than you realize.

* Here are some common hidden animal-based ingredients sometimes found in processed food: albumin, carminic acid (cochineal), casein, gelatin, lactose, lard, suet, rennet, and whey.

Supermarkets Are Full of Fantastic Food for Making Vegan Meals

There are so many wonderful vegan foods out there that you won't have enough time to taste all the possible combinations. With a basket of fresh fruits, vegetables, and whole grains, you're on your way to great vegan cooking. The staples listed here are suggestions for foods to have on hand. You don't need to stock all of them. Use the list for inspiration and a reminder when it's time to shop.

Beans   Canned beans are a must for quick vegan meals. For starters, buy garbanzo beans, navy beans, black beans, kidney beans, and pinto beans. They're all delicious! Dried beans are in-

expensive and easy to prepare. Start with the fast-cooking varieties: black-eyed peas, lentils, and split peas.

Baking Powder (aluminum-free) and Baking Soda   Check the
expiration date on the containers.

Canned Tomato Products   Keep canned whole tomatoes, diced
or crushed tomatoes, and tomato paste on hand. They form the
base for many meals.

Condiments   These "secret" ingredients add zest and instant flavor
by the spoonful. Hot sauce runs the gamut from mild to extreme,
and it can increase taste in everything from stir-fries to pasta
dishes. Mustards, salsas, and wasabi add punch to meals. Chipotle peppers in adobo sauce give a smoky flavor to sauces and
chili. Fresh lemon and lime juice add sparkle to meals, and a
splash of vinegar adds tang. Relish, chutneys, and hoisin sauce
bring spicy sweetness to recipes.

Dairy-free Milk   There are many varieties of vegan milk. Some
contain sweeteners, and some are flavored with chocolate, carob,
or vanilla. Taste and richness vary widely from brand to brand, so
experiment to find your number-one choice. You'll find nondairy
milk in the dairy case, as well as in shelf-stable aseptic packages.
Once opened, aseptic packages must be refrigerated and should
be used within seven to ten days.

Dried Fruit   Raisins and figs make a good beginning. When you
are ready for more, add dried dates, prunes, and apricots. Store
refrigerated in a closed container.

Drinks   Coffee, tea, cocoa powder, and juice.

Flour   Buy whole-grain flour and unbleached flours. Store all flour
in the refrigerator or freezer.

Fresh Vegetables   Onions, garlic, celery, and carrots are basic
cooking ingredients and are in a multitude of vegan recipes. Potatoes, sweet potatoes, and winter squash last for several weeks
stored in a cool, dry place and can become meals in themselves.

Onions give off gasses that make potatoes deteriorate quickly, so store them away from each other.

Frozen Vegetables   Look for quick-frozen vegetables sold in bags. The results are profoundly better than vegetables frozen in solid blocks. It's easy to reach into the package and use a handful at a time. Stay away from bags that are partially thawed or show evidence of having been thawed and refrozen—the telltale sign is a hard lump of vegetables rather than individual pieces. Corn, peas, soybeans, spinach, and bell peppers hold up well frozen. Add them to canned soups for a boost.

Fruit   Anytime is the right time for a colorful piece of fruit. Fruit adds a refreshing sparkle to your diet. Begin with the basics: apples, oranges, and bananas. They last longest refrigerated. Refrigerate bananas after they're flecked with brown specks to avoid overripening. The skins turn black in the refrigerator, but the fruit will taste fine. There are many wonderful kinds of fruit to try when you feel like branching out: papaya, kiwi, mango, pineapple, and more! Add fruit to salads and cereals. Use fresh or frozen fruit in smoothies.

Ginger   Ginger is a key ingredient in stir-fries and many other dishes. Keep fresh ginger tightly wrapped in plastic in the refrigerator. Peeling ginger is up to you; if it's fresh young ginger, don't bother. If the skin is older and thicker, you might want to peel it.

Herbs and Spices   For starters, consider black pepper, sea salt, cinnamon, cumin, curry, chili powder, red pepper flakes, oregano, rosemary, and thyme. The flavor and fragrance of herbs and spices fade over time, so buy them in small quantities, and store them away from heat in a cool, dry place.

Maple Syrup   Opt for pure maple syrup. It's expensive, but worth the price. Avoid products that contain corn syrup and artificial coloring.

Miso   Miso is a fermented product made from soybeans, salt, and various grains. Use it to give deep, rich flavor to chili, soups, marinara sauce, and vinaigrette dressings. Refrigerated it will keep for at least a year. White or rice miso is mild and relatively sweet. Dark miso is more strongly flavored.

Noodles   Great light-tasting whole-wheat Italian pastas are available in most markets and natural food groceries. Use rice, soba (buckwheat), and chewy udon noodles for meals with an Asian taste.

Nuts, Nut Butters, and Seeds   These small packages of protein add richness to vegan meals. For starters, consider buying walnuts and almonds, peanut butter and sesame tahini, sesame seeds and sunflower seeds. To keep the oil in nuts and nut butters fresh, store all nuts and seeds in the refrigerator or freezer in an airtight container. Untoasted nuts will keep for up to six months in the refrigerator, or for a year in the freezer. Nuts can be toasted ahead of time for recipes. Toasting nuts heightens their flavor, and they're crisper than untoasted nuts. They will keep for one to two weeks in the refrigerator, or for one to three months in the freezer.

Choose natural-style (nonhydrogenated) nut butter because it does not have trans-fatty acids. With nothing added to keep it emulsified, the oil tends to separate and float to the top of the jar. Stirring the oil back in takes work, but you can let gravity do it for you. Turn the jar upside down and leave the unopened jar on the countertop overnight. Once gravity mixes the oil back in, store the nut butter in the refrigerator.

Oils   Pure, fragrant olive oil is indispensable for cooking, and extra-virgin olive oil is good for salads. Avoid using extra-virgin olive oil for cooking, because it does not like high temperature and will smoke. Canola is a neutral, mild-flavored oil for cooking and baking. Store oil in the refrigerator to keep it from becoming rancid. The oil may solidify, but it will liquefy when brought to room temperature. If you're in a hurry, hold the bottle under hot running water.

Seaweed   Nori is one of many kinds of seaweed. It comes in packages of thin, flat sheets for making sushi. It's an interesting addition to soup and cooked grains. Lightly toasted, nori makes a tasty snack for nibbling. Store in a cool, dry place.

Shiitake Mushrooms (dried)   These versatile mushrooms add a rich, earthy flavor to soups, stews, and stir-fries.

Soy Sauce   Soy sauce is a dark brown liquid made from soybeans that have undergone a fermenting process. Look for naturally brewed soy sauce that does not contain sugar, food coloring, or chemical additives. Traditional Japanese soy sauce is made with wheat; tamari soy sauce is wheat-free.

Tortillas   These thin, unleavened flatbreads are made most simply from water mixed with wheat flour or corn flour. Look for brands with no added trans fat or preservatives in the dairy case or frozen-food aisle of the supermarket. Store them in the refrigerator or freezer.

Vegetable Broth   Using broth instead of water in some recipes adds extra flavor to your cooking. There are many different brands, and they taste markedly different from one another, so try several.

Whole Grains   For fast meals, become acquainted with quick-cooking grains such as polenta, quinoa, and couscous. Add whole-grain brown rice, oats, millet, and barley to your list. When you feel adventurous, branch out with buckwheat (kasha), red rice, black rice, or jasmine rice. For baking you will need whole-wheat flour and all-purpose unbleached white flour. Store all grains and breads in the refrigerator or freezer. Store granola in the refrigerator, too.

Meat Alternatives

A vegan diet doesn't mean you have to give up familiar tastes. You can savor meals of hearty chili, chicken potpies, and scrambled "eggs" by simply swapping tofu, tempeh, or seitan for meat. You may not be able to tell you've made the change because the flavors can be so similar.

Tofu   This is an extremely versatile, protein-rich food made from soybeans. Tofu is labeled soft, firm, or extra firm, depending on its water content. It comes fresh, packed in water-filled tubs, in vacuum packages, and in aseptic boxes. Use firm or extra-firm tofu for stir-fries, broiling, baking, and anytime you want tofu to hold its shape. Soft silken tofu, in aseptic packages, performs well in desserts, dressing, drinks, and dips. When purchasing tofu, always check the expiration date. Once you've opened a package of tofu, cover any leftovers with fresh water and refrigerate in a sealed container. Change the water every other day and the tofu will remain fresh for about five days.

Tempeh (TEM-pay)   Tempeh is a fermented, dense soybean cake, high in protein, with a pleasant, chewy texture. Some varieties are made entirely of soy, and others are mixed with one or more grains, giving it a mellower flavor. The recipes in this book use the mixed-grain variety. Look for tempeh in the refrigerated or frozen-food section of the supermarket. The unopened packages will keep refrigerated until the expiration date on the label. Once opened, tempeh should be tightly wrapped and used within three to four days. Tempeh may also be stored in the freezer for one month.

Seitan (SAY-tan)   When you prepare seitan in a meal, it's hard to tell that this meat alternative is not really meat. Seitan is made from gluten, the protein-rich part of wheat, and has been used for thousands of years in China and Japan. It is sold in quick-mix packages you prepare yourself, and in ready-to-use tubs or vacuum packs in a seasoned marinade. Look for seitan in most Asian markets and natural food stores. Seitan can be sliced for stir-fries and sautés, diced for soups and stews, and chopped and used in tacos or sandwich spreads.

Poaching tempeh before using it in a recipe tenderizes and mellows the flavor. Place the tempeh in a saucepan with water to cover, and simmer gently for 10 minutes. Then, remove it from the water and pat dry. It's ready to use. In dishes where tempeh simmers in liquid for 10 minutes or more, poaching is not important.

Thinking Inside the Box

Supermarket shelves and freezers are exploding with ready-to-eat vegan options: vegan cheese, burgers, lunch meat, hot dogs, ice cream, and more. So when you don't have time to cook, you'll find plenty to fill your plate.

Servings

A vegan diet consists of more grains, beans, fruits, and vegetables than the typical American diet. Use the servings in each recipe only as a guide, and decide for yourself how many servings you'll need for a healthy eating plan.

Tools

Professional chefs usually have an assortment of specialized tools and gadgets at their disposal. Many chefs, however, get by with a surprisingly small number of basic cooking tools and utensils: a good sauté skillet, a couple of sharp knives, a few pots and pans with lids, a baking sheet, a glass or ceramic casserole dish, a can opener, a spatula, a cutting board, and a large slotted spoon are the basics.

Next to a heat source, good knives are your most important kitchen tools. You don't need to break the bank on a knife, but you want one that will cut more than a vegan marshmallow. A serrated knife is also helpful for slicing bread, tomatoes, and snagging a pasta noodle in a pot of boiling water to test for doneness.

A number of kitchen procedures are made easier with some optional tools, but you can get by without them. A colander is helpful, but you can use a pot with its cover to drain vegetables and pasta. It's easy to skin a potato with a small knife instead of using a vegetable peeler. A fork can stand in for a wire whisk, although a wire whisk is fun to use. A small, inexpensive food processor is also useful.

Turning on the Heat

There is no single right way to cook. Cooking is also experimenting, and experiments lead to great discoveries. No matter how busy your day, everyone spends time eating, so let the recipes in this book stimulate you to use ingredients in new ways, and help you become familiar with fascinating ingredients you may have missed.

Measuring Equivalents

Pinch or dash	less than $1/8$ teaspoon
3 teaspoons	1 tablespoon
4 tablespoons	$1/4$ cup
1 cup	8 ounces
2 cups	1 pint
4 cups	1 quart
4 quarts	1 gallon
16 ounces	1 pound

Breakfast

You've heard it before—"Breakfast is the most important meal of the day." Ever wonder why? Studies show that people who eat breakfast have an easier time concentrating, are less likely to overeat during the course of the day, and have more strength and endurance in the late morning. There is also evidence that eating breakfast revs up your metabolism and increases the rate at which your body burns calories all day long.

If you don't have time to eat because you don't want to sacrifice sleep time, you may be onto something. The scientific literature on sleep points out that getting enough shut-eye also plays a big part in how a person feels and performs. To be alert, think clearly, and feel energetic, it may be necessary to eat breakfast *and* get a good night's sleep. The following fast-food breakfast ideas can help you do both.

Breakfast on the Go

- Spread a bagel with natural-style peanut butter.

- Morning is an ideal time to eat beans. They are protein-packed powerhouses that provide energy for hours. Cover a warm flour tortilla with refried beans, spoon on salsa, and roll it up for an easy carry-along meal. Top whole-grain toast with a helping of baked beans or chili.

- When you make whole-grain pancakes or waffles, make more than you need; freeze the extras and reheat them in a toaster for a fast meal.

- Cook more for dinner to create on-purpose leftovers, and eat them for breakfast.

- Whip up a fruit smoothie.

- Sip a cup of warm miso soup.

- Just about any fresh fruit can be eaten without utensils on the run.

- Enrich ready-to-eat cold cereal by adding sliced fresh fruit and nuts or seeds.

- Make a pot of hot cereal in the evening and refrigerate it. In the morning, spoon out a portion and reheat it in the microwave.

On those days when time permits some inventiveness in the morning, or there is a chance to share the pleasure of breakfast with friends, you'll find plenty to eat in this chapter.

Cereal Thriller— Irish Oatmeal with Apple Raisin Topping

PREPARATION TIME: 20 MINUTES

MAKES 2 SERVINGS

Corporations spend hundreds of thousands of dollars each day advertising rolled oats, so it's no surprise that's what most people choose. Fabulous Irish oatmeal is one of breakfast's best-kept secrets.

> 2 cups water or soy milk
> 1/2 cup Irish oatmeal (steel-cut oats)
> 1/8 teaspoon salt
> Apple Raisin Topping (recipe follows)

Bring the water to a boil in a saucepan. When the water boils, add the oats. Cook, uncovered, on medium, stirring occasionally for 10 to 15 minutes, or until creamy. Add the salt, lower the heat to medium-low, and continue cooking for 10 minutes (or to desired consistency), stirring occasionally to prevent sticking. To ensure a rich, nutty flavor, avoid overcooking. Remove from the heat and set aside for 2 to 3 minutes. Serve with Apple Raisin Topping.

VARIATION: For variety and something extra, add 1/4 cup well-rinsed quinoa to the pot when you add the oats. Quinoa contributes a unique flavor along with extra calcium and B vitamins.

Apple Raisin Topping

PREPARATION TIME: 15 MINUTES
MAKES 2 SERVINGS

There is no more heavenly aroma in the world of cooking than apples mixed with cinnamon.

- 1 apple, quartered, cored, and cut into bite-size pieces
- 1/4 cup raisins
- 1 teaspoon brown or white sugar, or natural sweetener
- 2 tablespoons orange juice, apple juice, or water
- 1/4 teaspoon ground cinnamon

In a medium pot, combine the ingredients; bring to a low boil and simmer on medium-low heat for about 10 minutes, until the apple pieces are soft, stirring occasionally.

Oatmeal

Steel-cut oats—also called Irish oatmeal—are made from unprocessed oat groats that have been cut into pieces with steel blades. They take about 20 minutes to prepare. When you want oatmeal with amazing flavor and a chewy texture, steel-cut oats top the list.

Rolled oats—also called regular or old-fashioned oats—are made from oat groats that have been steamed and flattened with giant rollers. They take about 10 minutes to prepare and make a substantial, creamy bowl of oatmeal.

Quick-cooking oats and instant oats take only a few minutes to prepare, but they turn into something more like wallpaper paste when cooked, and they're better left on the supermarket shelf.

18   *Student's Go Vegan Cookbook*

Walnut and Fig Old-Fashioned Oatmeal

PREPARATION TIME: 10 MINUTES
MAKES 1 SERVING

A bowl of steaming oatmeal is the ideal medium for topping with sliced fresh fruit or bits of dried fruit. Bananas are a good choice because they're cheap and available year-round. This recipe includes dried figs, a fruit high in calcium.

1 cup water
Pinch of salt
1/2 cup rolled oats
1 or 2 chopped dried figs
1 to 2 tablespoons toasted walnuts, chopped*
1 to 2 teaspoons pure maple syrup (optional)

Bring the water and salt to a boil in a small saucepan over high heat. Stir in the oats and reduce the heat to low. Cover and gently simmer for about 5 minutes, until the oatmeal is smooth and creamy, stirring occasionally to keep the oats from sticking. Remove from heat and stir in the figs. Cover and let rest for 2 to 3 minutes. Spoon the oatmeal into a bowl, sprinkle with walnuts, drizzle with maple syrup, and serve.

*NOTE: Place the nuts in a small, dry skillet over medium heat. Stir the nuts or shake the pan constantly for 3 to 5 minutes, or until fragrant and lightly browned. Remove the nuts from the skillet immediately to stop the cooking process. Nuts can be toasted ahead of time and will keep in an airtight container for one to two weeks in the refrigerator, or for one to three months in the freezer.

3-Minute Microwave Oatmeal

For 1 serving of regular or old-fashioned oatmeal, put 1 cup water and $1/2$ cup oats in a large 4-cup or larger microwavable container. Oats get rowdy in a microwave and can boil over, so make sure you use a big container. Cook on high for $2^1/2$ to 3 minutes. Remove from the microwave and let it sit until it's cool enough to eat. Stir before serving.

If you're wondering whether a container is microwave-safe, there's an easy way to test it. Pour 1 cup of water into the container. Place it in the microwave on full power for 1 minute. If the water gets hot and the container stays cool, it is safe to use. If the container gets hot, it may contain lead or metals and shouldn't be used in the microwave.

Pineapple-Ginger Oatmeal

Pineapple and the peppery taste of fresh ginger combine for an unusual breakfast. The oatmeal is made without turning on the stove, and it is steeped in nondairy milk.

$1/2$ cup old-fashioned rolled oats
$1/4$ cup canned, unsweetened crushed pineapple
$1/2$ cup nondairy milk
$1/2$ to 1 teaspoon finely chopped fresh ginger

In a medium bowl, combine the oats, pineapple, nondairy milk, and ginger. Stir well, cover, and refrigerate for several hours, or overnight. Serve the oatmeal topped with additional fresh fruit, such as bananas, strawberries, or sliced peaches, if you like.

The Pots Come Clean

Soaking the pot you use for cooking oatmeal (or soaking any pot used to cook grain) will make it easier to clean later; it's even faster than cleaning it right away.

Tofu Scramble Asian-Style

Serve this calcium-rich scramble with toast or a muffin and a cup of jasmine tea.

Sauce
- 1 teaspoon light miso
- 1 teaspoon warm water
- 1 teaspoon soy sauce
- Splash of dark sesame oil

Tofu Scramble
- 4 ounces soft tofu
- 1 1/2 teaspoons toasted sesame seeds
- 2 cups stemmed, sliced Swiss chard (about 2 or 3 leaves)
- 1 tablespoon olive oil
- 1/4 cup chopped onions
- 1 garlic clove, minced
- 1 teaspoon minced fresh ginger
- Red pepper flakes or Tabasco sauce

In a small bowl, mix the miso with the warm water until smooth. Stir in the soy sauce and sesame oil. Set aside.

Place the tofu between two plates and rest a heavy book or weight on the top plate. Press for 15 minutes, then drain the expressed liquid from the bottom plate.

Toast the sesame seeds in a dry skillet over moderate heat for 3 to 5 minutes, stirring as needed to keep them from burning, until they are fragrant and golden. Set aside.

Wash the chard and do not dry. The water that clings to the leaves helps them cook. Stack the leaves and roll them lengthwise into a long cigar shape, then cut the leaves crosswise to produce ribbons of greens.

Heat the oil in a medium skillet on medium heat. Add the onions and sauté for 2 to 3 minutes, or until they begin to soften. Add the garlic, ginger, and chard. Sauté until the greens begin to wilt. Cover and continue cooking for about 5 minutes, until the greens are just tender. Crumble the pressed tofu into the vegetables. Cook the vegetables and tofu, uncovered, for 4 to 5 minutes without stirring, until the moisture evaporates. Turn the mixture and cook for 2 more minutes. Turn off the heat.

Pour the sauce over the scramble and gently stir. Serve sprinkled with sesame seeds. Add a shake of red pepper flakes or a few drops of Tabasco sauce if you like.

Tofu Scramble Burrito-Style

PREPARATION TIME: 20 MINUTES
MAKES 3 SERVINGS

Tofu seasoned with chili powder and cumin makes a perfect filling for a Mexican wrap.

    8 ounces soft tofu
    1 tablespoon olive oil
    1/2 cup diced yellow onion
    1 garlic clove, minced
    1/2 cup diced bell pepper
    1 teaspoon ground cumin
    1 teaspoon chili powder
    1/2 teaspoon salt
    3 regular (6-inch) whole-wheat flour tortillas
    Salsa
    1 tablespoon minced fresh parsley or fresh cilantro

Sandwich the tofu between two plates and rest a heavy book or weight on the top plate. Press for 15 minutes, then drain the expressed liquid from the bottom plate.

In a medium skillet on medium heat, warm the oil. Add the onions and sauté for 3 to 5 minutes, until they begin to soften. Add the garlic, bell pepper, cumin, chili powder, and salt.

Crumble the pressed tofu into the skillet and stir gently to combine the tofu with the vegetables. Cook for about 4 minutes, uncovered, until the moisture evaporates. Gently turn the scramble and continue cooking for another 2 to 3 minutes.

Warm the tortillas in a dry skillet over medium to medium-high heat for a minute. Spoon the filling into the center of each tortilla and top with salsa and cilantro or parsley. Fold the burrito: first bring the bottom end over the filling, and then fold in the sides to create a package with one end open. Serve hot.

Tofu "Bacon" Scramble

PREPARATION TIME: 20 MINUTES
MAKES 1 SERVING

This recipe uses Fakin' Bacon, a product made from tempeh. Its assertive flavor adds a smoky taste to the dish. If it is unavailable, substitute crumbled vegan sausage, or a chopped vegan veggie burger. The turmeric turns the scramble bright yellow (just for fun, try adding a pinch or two to a pot of rice while it cooks).

4 ounces soft tofu
2 teaspoons olive oil
Pinch of turmeric
$1/4$ cup (2 slices) crumbled Fakin' Bacon
1 teaspoon chopped scallion
$1/8$ to $1/4$ cup chopped tomato
Salt and ground black pepper
Fresh chopped parsley

To press the tofu, place the tofu between two plates and rest a heavy book or weight on the top plate. Press for 15 minutes, then drain the expressed liquid from the bottom plate.

Crumble the tofu into a bowl. Heat the oil in a medium skillet on medium heat. Add the tofu and turmeric. Stir until the tofu is the color of scrambled eggs. Add the Fakin' Bacon, scallion, and tomato. Continue cooking for 1 to 2 minutes, or until the scramble is warm. Salt and pepper to taste. Sprinkle with parsley and serve.

Making Carefree Pancakes

Active baking powder and baking soda make pancakes rise, but sometimes these two ingredients sit on the shelf too long and lose their power. Check the expiration date on the boxes.

For light, fluffy pancakes, combine the wet and dry ingredients with a few quick strokes. It's better to leave some lumps than to stir too much. After mixing, let the batter rest for a few minutes to give the baking powder or baking soda a chance to work. You'll know it's ready when you see tiny bubbles on the surface. The batter should be medium-thick but still pourable. If the batter becomes too thick while it stands, stir in a tablespoon or more liquid. If it's too runny, stir in a tablespoon or two more flour.

Heat the pan well before cooking the pancakes. When a drop of water sizzles, and before the oil in the pan smokes, the pan is ready to use. To give pancakes a professional look and a uniform size, ladle the batter into the skillet from a $\frac{1}{4}$ cup measuring cup.

For the best pancakes, turn them only once, and don't flatten or level them with the spatula. If the pancakes become too brown before they're ready to turn, lower the heat. If they're too light, raise the heat slightly.

Keep the pancakes warm in a 200°F oven in a single layer on a baking sheet; stacked pancakes become soggy if kept waiting. If you're not using them right away, cool the pancakes completely and refrigerate or freeze them. When you want more, defrost and reheat the pancakes in a toaster or toaster oven.

Crunchy Blueberry Pancakes

When you have time for relaxing and lingering over a cup of coffee, mix up a batch of light and elegant vegan pancakes and consider inviting a friend for breakfast. Cornmeal gives the pancakes extra crunch, and adding the blueberries while the pancakes cook keeps the batter from turning blue. Serve drizzled with pure maple syrup.

1 1/4 cup whole-wheat pastry flour
1/2 cup cornmeal
1/4 teaspoon salt
1/2 teaspoon baking soda
1/2 teaspoon baking powder
1/2 teaspoon ground cinnamon
1 1/3 cups soy milk
2 tablespoons pure maple syrup
1 1/2 tablespoons freshly squeezed lemon juice
3 tablespoons canola oil
1/2 cup fresh or frozen blueberries, thawed

In a large bowl, combine the flour, cornmeal, salt, baking soda, baking powder, and cinnamon.

In a medium bowl, combine the soy milk, maple syrup, lemon juice, and oil. Pour the soy milk mixture into the flour mixture. Stir just to combine.

Heat a lightly oiled skillet over medium-high heat. For each pancake, ladle 1/4 cup of the batter onto the skillet. Sprinkle the top of each pancake with blueberries. When bubbles begin to appear on the top of the pancakes, after about 1 to 1 1/2 minutes, turn, and cook until the second side is golden.

Banana-Walnut Pancakes

These pancakes have a sweet, light banana flavor. Serve them with sliced strawberries, pure maple syrup, or blueberry syrup.

$3/4$ cup unbleached all-purpose flour*
$1/4$ cup whole-wheat flour*
$1/4$ teaspoon salt
2 teaspoons baking powder
$1/4$ teaspoon ground cinnamon
$1/4$ cup finely chopped toasted walnuts**
$1/4$ cup rolled oats
$1 1/3$ cups soy milk
1 tablespoon canola oil
1 tablespoon pure maple syrup
1 large banana, sliced (about 1 cup)

In a large bowl, combine the two flours, salt, baking powder, cinnamon, and nuts. Mix well. Stir in the oats.

In a separate bowl, combine the soy milk, oil, and maple syrup. Pour the soy milk mixture into the flour mixture. Stir just to combine. Fold in the banana slices.

Lightly oil a medium skillet and place on medium to medium-high heat. Use $1/2$ cup of batter for each pancake and cook until bubbles appear on top. Flip the pancakes as soon as the bubbles start to form to avoid scorching them. Cook for 1 minute, or until the second side is lightly browned. If the batter becomes thick as it stands, stir in more soy milk, a tablespoon or two at a time.

*NOTE: You can reverse the flour proportions and use $3/4$ cup whole-wheat flour and $1/4$ cup unbleached all-purpose flour if you prefer. You'll need to add more soy milk to make a creamy batter.

**NOTE: Toast the nuts on an unoiled baking sheet in a preheated 350°F oven for 3 to 5 minutes, or until fragrant and lightly browned. Remove immediately from the sheet to stop the cooking process. When the nuts are cool, chop and set aside. Nuts can be toasted ahead of time and will keep in an airtight container for one to two weeks in the refrigerator, or for one to three months in the freezer.

Apple-Pecan French Toast

PREPARATION TIME: 15 MINUTES
MAKES 2 SERVINGS

Forget coffee-shop sticky buns and consider starting the day with whole-grain French toast mounded with applesauce and sprinkled with toasted pecans. To save time in the morning, the bread slices can be soaked in the batter the night before and refrigerated, covered, until morning. This recipe uses a blender, but if you don't have one, a fork or wire whisk works. The dipping mixture won't be as smooth, but it will taste the same.

$3/4$ cup soy milk or dairy-free milk
2 ounces soft silken tofu, drained
$1/2$ teaspoon pure vanilla extract
2 tablespoons pure maple syrup
4 slices whole-grain bread
Applesauce
$1/3$ cup toasted pecans, chopped*

Combine the soy milk, tofu, vanilla, and maple syrup in a blender and process until smooth. Pour the mixture into a large, shallow bowl and dip in the bread. Soak the slices for 2 minutes, turning them once to coat both sides.

Lightly oil a medium skillet and place on medium-high heat. Add the bread and cook for 4 to 5 minutes, or until lightly browned on both sides.

Serve hot, topped with the applesauce and chopped nuts.

*NOTE: Toast the nuts on an unoiled baking sheet in a preheated 350°F oven for 3 to 5 minutes, or until fragrant and lightly browned. Remove immediately from the sheet to stop the cooking process. When the nuts are cool, chop and set aside. Nuts can be toasted ahead of time and will keep in an airtight container for one to two weeks in the refrigerator, or for one to three months in the freezer.

NOTE: If your skillet is not large enough to cook 4 slices of toast at once, keep finished toast warm in a 200°F oven while you prepare the remaining slices.

Hash in a Flash

This colorful "flash-in-a-pan" vegetable and sausage dish is both sweet and savory. It's not necessary to peel the potato, but you can if you like.

2 tablespoons olive oil
1 cup sweet potato (diced into $1/2$-inch pieces)
$1/2$ cup chopped yellow onion
$1/2$ cup diced bell pepper (red or green)
$1 1/3$ cups thawed and chopped frozen vegan sausage patties or vegan burgers
$1/4$ to $1/2$ teaspoon red pepper flakes
Salt and ground black pepper

Preheat the oven to 400°F. To a medium bowl, add 1 tablespoon of oil. Toss the potatoes with the oil until well coated. Sprinkle the potatoes in a single layer onto a baking sheet and bake until tender, about 15 minutes. Stir once.

When the potatoes are ready, heat 1 tablespoon of oil in a medium skillet on medium heat. Add the onion and bell pepper and sauté for 3 to 4 minutes, or until the vegetables are tender, stirring frequently. Add the potatoes, sausage, red pepper flakes, salt, and pepper. Cook, stirring frequently, for 5 minutes, or until the potatoes are lightly browned. Serve immediately.

Cinnamon-Maple Granola

PREPARATION TIME: 10 MINUTES
BAKING TIME: 20 MINUTES
MAKES 4 CUPS

The aroma of granola toasting in the oven might get your room-mates up early for breakfast. You may never want to eat store-bought granola again when you see how simple it is to make. Serve the granola in a bowl and pour on some nondairy milk, or eat it right out of your hand for a quick snack. It makes a crunchy topping on sliced fresh fruit and vegan ice cream.

2$\frac{1}{2}$ cups rolled oats
$\frac{1}{4}$ cup chopped or slivered almonds
$\frac{1}{3}$ cup chopped walnuts
$\frac{1}{4}$ cup sunflower seeds
2 tablespoons cashews
$\frac{1}{3}$ cup pure maple syrup
$\frac{1}{4}$ cup canola or safflower oil
1 teaspoon ground cinnamon
$\frac{1}{8}$ teaspoon salt
$\frac{1}{3}$ cup raisins

Preheat the oven to 350°F.

Combine all the ingredients, except the raisins, in a large bowl. Stir to coat with oil. Spread the mixture out on a lightly oiled baking sheet and bake for 20 minutes until golden, stirring every 5 minutes. Granola cooks quickly, so watch it carefully so it does not burn.

Remove from the oven and stir occasionally to dispel the heat. When completely cooled, add the raisins. Transfer to an airtight container. It will keep for 3 weeks.

VARIATION: You can substitute dried cherries, cranberries, figs, or apples for the raisins to vary the flavor of the granola. Dried fruit burns easily, so always add it after the granola is removed from the oven.

Hot Pocket Mushroom Sauté

PREPARATION TIME: 15 MINUTES
MAKES 2 SERVINGS

You might be surprised to know that the small brown cremini mushrooms sold in most supermarkets are baby portobellos. They taste great, and they're a lot cheaper.

8 ounces cremini mushrooms
1 tablespoon olive oil
1 large garlic clove, minced
Pinch of salt
1 tablespoon fresh lemon juice
1 1/2 teaspoons balsamic vinegar
Pinch of sugar or natural sweetener
2 tablespoons chopped fresh parsley or fresh cilantro
Salt and ground black pepper
1 whole-grain pocket bread cut in half

Brush off any soil that clings to the mushrooms with a dry paper towel, then thinly slice. In a medium skillet on medium-high, heat the oil and add the mushrooms, garlic, and salt. Sear until well-browned and slightly softened for 4 to 5 minutes, turning occasionally. Add the lemon juice, balsamic vinegar, and sugar, turning to coat; cook for another 3 to 5 minutes.

Stir in the parsley. Remove from heat. Add salt and pepper to taste. Scoop into a warm whole-grain pocket bread and serve immediately.

Bagel Tahini Carrot Spread

Use this spread on bagels or crackers sprinkled with chopped scallions or raisins. If you're up for a peppery start to the day, add chopped watercress.

    ¹/₄ cup light miso
    ¹/₄ cup toasted sesame tahini
    ¹/₄ cup shredded carrots

Combine all of the ingredients in a bowl. Use immediately, or refrigerate, covered. The spread keeps for 5 days.

Snacks and Dips

The snacks and dips in this chapter are nutritious as well as tasty, so forget the mantra "Don't snack or you'll ruin your appetite." That's the point of eating, and healthy snacks play an important part in your daily diet. With the smallest of effort you'll have healthful options that can sometimes become mini-meals.

Basic Baked Tofu

PREPARATION TIME: 10 MINUTES
TOFU PRESSING TIME: 20 MINUTES
TOFU MARINATING TIME: ABOUT 3 HOURS
BAKING TIME: 30 TO 45 MINUTES
MAKES ABOUT 4 SERVINGS

Baked tofu makes a welcome snack for nibbling and a tasty sandwich filling. Try it warm, cut into cubes with baked vegetables or grain dishes. It's also great cold, sliced, and tossed into green salads. Baked tofu is readily available in most natural food stores; however, making it yourself costs a lot less. In this recipe, the tofu is marinated for several hours and removed from the marinade to bake.

    1 block (16 ounces) firm tofu

Marinade
    $1/3$ cup soy sauce
    1 tablespoon toasted sesame oil
    2 tablespoons fresh lemon juice
    3 tablespoons water
    2 tablespoons finely minced fresh ginger
    1 tablespoon finely minced garlic
    $1/8$ to $1/4$ teaspoon red pepper flakes

Preheat the oven to 375°F.

Sandwich the tofu between two plates and rest a heavy book or weight on the top plate. Press for 15 to 20 minutes, then drain the liquid. Cut the tofu into $1/2$-inch-thick slices.

Use the smallest glass baking dish you have that will hold the slices of tofu in a single layer. Combine all of the marinade ingredients in the baking dish. Add the tofu. Cover and refrigerate for 1 hour. Turn the slices and continue marinating 2 hours longer.

(continued)

Remove the tofu from the marinade and place it on a lightly oiled baking sheet. Bake for 30 to 45 minutes, turning the tofu once after 30 minutes. The longer the tofu bakes, the chewier it becomes. Serve at once or let it cool and store in a tightly sealed container in the refrigerator for 3 to 4 days.

Rosemary-Lemon Baked Tofu

PREPARATION TIME: 7 MINUTES
TOFU PRESSING TIME: 20 MINUTES
BAKING TIME: 30 TO 60 MINUTES
MAKES ABOUT 4 SERVINGS

Tofu soaks up the flavor of whatever marinade you choose. In this recipe, tofu has a bright, lemony flavor. Use it as a between-meal snack, or serve it with a plate of stir-fried vegetables. The tofu goes directly into the oven and marinates and bakes at the same time.

1 block (16 ounces) firm tofu

Marinade
1 teaspoon minced lemon zest*
$^1/_4$ cup fresh lemon juice (about 1 medium lemon)
2 tablespoons soy sauce
3 tablespoons olive oil
1 tablespoon minced fresh rosemary or 1 teaspoon dried
   and crumbled rosemary
$^1/_4$ teaspoon ground black pepper

Preheat the oven to 375°F.
Sandwich the block of tofu between two plates and rest a heavy book or weight on the top plate. Press for about 20 to 25 minutes, then drain the liquid.
Cut the tofu horizontally into 4 slices (each about $^1/_2$ inch thick).
Use the smallest glass baking dish you have that will hold the slices of tofu in a single layer (an 8-inch square pan or 7 × 9-inch pan both work fine). Combine all of the marinade ingredients in the baking dish. Add the tofu, and turn the slices to coat both sides.

(continued)

Bake for 30 to 60 minutes, turning once about halfway through. The longer the tofu bakes, the chewier it becomes. Serve immediately or let it cool and store in a tightly sealed container in the refrigerator for 3 to 4 days.

*NOTE: Use a vegetable peeler or sharp knife to shave off the thin, bright yellow skin of the lemon, taking care not to peel off the bitter whitish tissue under the rind. If you are uncertain of the source of the fruit (whether it's organic or not), use hot water to remove whatever may have been sprayed on the surface.

Thai Spring Rolls with Spicy Peanut Dipping Sauce

PREPARATION TIME: 10 TO 15 MINUTES

MAKES 1 SERVING (4 ROLLS)

Fresh, uncooked Thai spring rolls make sublime snacks or a light lunch. The wrappers are made from rice flour and look like translucent wafers in the package. They are brittle, so handle them gently. They come round and square, large and small. Large wrappers are easier to roll than small ones. Look for them in Asian markets and well-stocked supermarkets.

Package directions advise you to briefly soak the wrappers in a shallow pan of warm water. Briefly is the operative word. Soak them one at a time, or they'll stick together. Judging the exact amount of filling for each roll comes with a little practice. It's better to put on too little filling than too much, because rolls that are too full are difficult to roll and more likely to split open. (If a roll splits, put it on another softened wrapper and roll it up again for a double wrap.) Once you've made two or three rolls, you'll be a professional. Honest.

Spring rolls are best eaten soon after they are prepared but will keep for several hours in the refrigerator in a tightly sealed container. Vary the filling ingredients according to what you have on hand and your personal tastes.

2 round spring roll wrappers (about 8½ inches in diameter)

Filling
About 1½ cups shredded lettuce
About ⅓ cup thinly sliced carrots (lengthwise)
About ½ avocado, thinly sliced

(continued)

About ¼ cup thinly sliced cucumber
2 to 4 fresh basil leaves, thinly sliced

Submerge one wrapper in a large, shallow pan of warm water; slowly turn it in the water with your fingers until it is pliable, about 30 to 60 seconds. You'll feel it softening under your fingertips. Carefully transfer the wrapper to a clean kitchen towel or flat work surface, and gently pat dry. Note: The wrapper will continue to soften after removing it from the water.

Arrange a small amount of each of the filling ingredients in a horizontal line on the bottom third of the wrapper. Fold the bottom edge over the filling toward the center, roll once to capture the filling, then fold in the two side edges of the wrapper and continue rolling up the package like a sleeping bag. Slice the roll in half with a sharp knife (it looks prettiest if you make a diagonal cut). Place seam side down on a serving plate. Repeat with the remaining wrapper. Serve with dipping sauce.

More Filling Possibilities:

Shredded napa or Chinese cabbage

Thinly sliced scallions

Thinly sliced radishes

Thinly sliced red bell pepper

Chopped fresh mint leaves

Chopped fresh cilantro

Thinly sliced fresh pineapple

Thinly sliced fresh mango

Chopped unsalted, dry-roasted peanuts

Cooked vermicelli rice noodles (follow package directions)

Lightly sautéed fresh tofu (add only one or two thinly sliced strips to each roll)

Spicy Peanut Dipping Sauce

MAKES $\frac{1}{3}$ CUP

2 tablespoons natural-style peanut butter
1 teaspoon brown sugar or natural sweetener
1 tablespoon fresh lemon juice
$1\frac{1}{2}$ tablespoons salsa
1 to $1\frac{1}{2}$ teaspoons hot water

Combine ingredients in a small bowl.

Simple Dipping Sauce

MAKES ABOUT $\frac{1}{3}$ CUP

2 teaspoons brown sugar or natural sweetener
2 tablespoons soy sauce
1 tablespoon rice vinegar, fresh lime juice, or fresh lemon juice

Combine ingredients in a small bowl.

Lettuce Wraps

Lettuce leaves make convenient wrappers for interesting fillings made from small pieces of fresh or cooked vegetables, nuts, beans, rice, and grains. Wraps are also a speedy way to use up bits of leftovers and make them shine. Almost anything goes, but keep the pieces small enough so they're easy to bite. A lettuce leaf the size of the palm of your hand makes a good beginning. Soft green lettuce such as butter and Bibb work well for folding into packages. Romaine is good for rolling into burrito-style wraps. Part of the pleasure of making wraps is designing them with a touch of your favorite condiments. Dipping sauces are tasty, but optional. Here are two filling ideas to get you started.

White Bean Filling

FILLS 2 TO 3 WRAPS

¼ cup cooked white beans
Splash of fresh lemon juice
Splash of olive oil
3 to 4 teaspoons finely chopped fresh mint
Salt and ground black pepper to taste

2 lettuce leaves, washed and dried

Combine the ingredients in a small bowl. Spoon the filling onto the lettuce leaf, roll it, and pop it into your mouth.

Curried Tempeh Filling

3 to 4 ounces (about $1/2$ cup) multigrain tempeh*
$3/4$ cup apple juice
1 tablespoon vegan mayonnaise
$1^1/2$ tablespoons toasted, chopped walnuts**
$1/8$ to $1/4$ teaspoon curry powder
$1/2$ teaspoon fresh lemon juice
1 teaspoon finely chopped scallion
2 teaspoons raisins or mango chutney

2 or 3 lettuce leaves, washed and dried

In a small saucepan, simmer the tempeh in the apple juice, covered, for 20 minutes. When cool, put the tempeh in a medium bowl and mash and crumble it with a fork. Add the vegan mayonnaise, walnuts, curry powder, lemon juice, scallions, and raisins. Stir to combine. Spread the mixture onto the center of each leaf and roll into a package—they're ready to eat. For something extra, dip the wrap into sweet Asian hoisin sauce.

*NOTE: Tempeh comes in several mixtures. Multigrain tempeh has a mild taste. If you're new to using tempeh, please start with this variety.

**NOTE: Place the nuts in a small, dry skillet over medium heat. Stir the nuts or shake the pan constantly for 3 to 5 minutes, until fragrant and lightly browned. Remove the nuts from the skillet immediately to stop the cooking process. Nuts can be toasted ahead of time and will keep in an airtight container for 1 to 2 weeks in the refrigerator, or for 1 to 3 months in the freezer.

Toasted Pumpkin Seeds

PREPARATION TIME: 10 MINUTES
MAKES ¹/₂ CUP

Put toasted pumpkin seeds in a bowl and see how fast they disappear. Sweet Maple Flavored Pumpkin Seeds are great for munching with a sliced apple or juicy pear. Try sprinkling savory Smoky Flavored Pumpkin Seeds in soups or salads.

Maple Flavored
$^1/_2$ cup raw pumpkin seeds
$1^1/_2$ teaspoons pure maple syrup
$^1/_8$ to $^1/_4$ teaspoon cayenne pepper
Pinch of salt

Smoky Flavored
$^1/_2$ cup raw pumpkin seeds
1 teaspoon olive oil
$^1/_2$ teaspoon salt
$^1/_4$ teaspoon chipotle chili powder

Preheat oven to 350°F.

Choose a flavor and toss the ingredients together in a small bowl until the seeds are well coated. Spread the seeds on a lightly oiled baking sheet and bake for 5 minutes, or until the seeds are lightly browned or just begin to pop. Remove the seeds from the pan, and cool for a minute or two.

Vegetable Pancakes with Sesame Sauce

PREPARATION TIME: 5 MINUTES
COOKING TIME: ABOUT 7 MINUTES FOR EACH PANCAKE
MAKES 2 PANCAKES

Cut the savory pancakes into wedges and drizzle with Sesame Sauce. Then brew up a cup of hot green tea and dig into a soothing snack.

$1/2$ cup whole-wheat flour
$1/4$ teaspoon baking powder
$1/8$ teaspoon salt
$1/2$ cup water
1 teaspoon canola oil
1 tablespoon sesame seeds
1 mushroom, thinly sliced
4 scallions ($1/2$ cup), thinly sliced

In a medium bowl, stir or whisk the flour, baking powder, and salt. Add the water. Stir with a fork until just blended. The batter should be medium-thick. If necessary, add more water, 1 to 2 tablespoons at a time. Let the batter rest for a minute to allow the baking powder to begin forming bubbles on the surface.

Heat $1/2$ teaspoon oil in a medium skillet on medium heat. When a drop of water sizzles on the surface, the skillet is ready. Ladle $1/2$ cup of the batter into the skillet. Sprinkle the top of the pancake with half of the sesame seeds, lightly press half of the mushrooms onto the surface, and scatter half of the scallions on top. Use a spatula to gently press the topping into the pancake.

Cook for 3 to 4 minutes, or until lightly browned on the bottom side. Then flip the pancake, and cook for 2 to 3 minutes more, until the vegetables are lightly browned.

For the second pancake, repeat with the remaining oil, batter, and vegetables. Serve immediately, drizzled with Sesame Sauce.

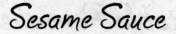

Sesame Sauce

You can also use this sauce spooned over steamed vegetables.

2 tablespoons soy sauce
1 tablespoon rice vinegar
1 tablespoon fresh lemon juice
1 1/2 teaspoons toasted sesame oil

Combine the ingredients in a small bowl. The sauce will keep refrigerated for a week.

VARIATIONS: Add minced ginger, minced garlic, a dash of red pepper flakes, or a pinch of brown sugar or natural sweetener to give the sauce a little extra kick. If you desire, add all four.

Energy Orbs with Dates and Walnuts

PREPARATION TIME: 25 MINUTES
MAKES ABOUT THIRTY 1/2-INCH BALLS

Energy bars are a hot item at the grocery store. Some contain wholesome ingredients, but most are loaded with high-fructose corn syrup, caffeine, and palm kernel oil—an oil that has twice the saturated fat of lard. This recipe is a melt-in-your-mouth alternative to commercial bars. The date variety you'll most often find available are the smooth deglet noor. If you see any large, crinkly-skinned medjool dates, they're divine, so try them, too.

1 1/2 cups dates, pitted
1 1/2 cups toasted walnuts*
1 teaspoon pure vanilla extract
2 tablespoons unsweetened cocoa powder (optional)
About 1/2 to 3/4 cup unsweetened, finely shredded coconut
    (optional)

Soak the pitted dates in hot water for about 10 minutes. Drain well.
    In a food processor, grind the toasted nuts into small pieces, until they're almost a powder. Add the dates, vanilla, and cocoa powder, if using. Puree well; the mixture will look like thick cookie dough.
    Scrape the "dough" into a medium bowl. Roll pieces into 1/2-inch round balls with the palms of your hands. Put the coconut into a shallow cup, and then roll the balls in the coconut to coat. Store in a covered container in the refrigerator. They will keep for 2 weeks, but they're so tempting they probably won't last that long.

(continued)

*NOTE: Toast the nuts on a dry baking sheet in a preheated 350°F. oven for 5 to 6 minutes, or until fragrant and lightly browned. Remove immediately from the pan to stop the cooking process. Cool for 5 minutes.

NOTE: It's easiest to make this recipe using a food processor, but a blender also works. If using a blender, combine the mixture in three batches. First process 1/2 cup nuts, then add 1/2 cup dates, a dash of vanilla, and about 1/2 teaspoon unsweetened cocoa powder, and whirl into a thick "dough." Transfer to a bowl, and repeat the process with the remaining ingredients. Roll the mixture into balls with the palms of your hands, and then roll the balls in the coconut.

Black-Eyed Pea Salsa

PREPARATION TIME: 5 MINUTES
MAKES ABOUT 1^1/$_2$ CUPS

These legumes are traditionally eaten in the South for good fortune in the new year. Each pea sports a black "eye" at the inner curve. This recipe is open to interpretation; use it as salsa with chips or serve it as a salad. The lime juice complements the natural sweetness of black-eyed peas.

1 cup canned black-eyed peas, drained
2 tablespoons canned mild green chilies
1 tomato, finely chopped
1 scallion, finely sliced
Juice from half a lime
^{1}/$_8$ teaspoon salt
Tabasco to taste

Combine all of the ingredients in a bowl, and serve with tortilla chips.

NOTE: If you have the time, consider cooking dried black-eyed peas instead of using the canned variety. Dried black-eyed peas do not require presoaking. Cover ^{1}/$_2$ cup black-eyed peas with an inch or two of water. Bring the pot to a boil, and simmer for 45 to 50 minutes, or until the beans are tender.

Avocado and Orange Salsa

PREPARATION TIME: 7 MINUTES
MAKES ABOUT 1 CUP

The avocado and orange make this fresh salsa mellow and sweet. It's perfect with any simple bean dish and also goes great with Lickety-Split Burger Hash (page 169).

$^1/_2$ medium navel orange
$^1/_4$ cup peeled, diced cucumber
$^1/_2$ jalapeño pepper, seeded and minced
2 tablespoons minced red onion
2 tablespoons chopped cilantro
1 tablespoon fresh lime juice
Salt
$^1/_4$ cup peeled, diced avocado

Peel the orange, removing any white pith with a sharp knife, and chop it into bite-size pieces. In a medium bowl, combine the orange, cucumber, jalapeño pepper, red onion, cilantro, lime juice, and salt. Add the avocado, and toss gently to mix.

Fresh Cilantro Dip

PREPARATION TIME: 8 MINUTES
MAKES 3/4 CUP

This light green dip works great with chips. Try spooning it on tacos, too.

> 4 ounces soft silken tofu
> 1 cup finely chopped fresh cilantro
> 1 or 2 garlic cloves, minced
> 1/2 jalapeño pepper, seeded and finely chopped
> 1 1/2 teaspoons olive oil
> 1 to 2 tablespoons lime juice
> Salt and ground black pepper

Combine all the ingredients in a blender or whip with a wire whisk or fork in a bowl until smooth.

Mediterranean Eggplant Spread

The proportions for this recipe are flexible, so taste as you mix. Brush crusty slices of artisan bread with olive oil, and toast the slices in a warm skillet until lightly browned. Spoon the spread onto the bread and serve. The spread keeps for several days in the refrigerator.

  1 firm, shiny eggplant (about 1 1/4 pounds)
  1 tablespoon olive oil
  1/2 medium onion, finely chopped
  2 garlic cloves, minced
  2 medium tomatoes, chopped
  1/4 cup chopped fresh basil leaves
  1/4 cup chopped fresh flat-leaf parsley leaves
  3 tablespoons fresh lemon juice
  1/2 teaspoon sugar or natural sweetener
  Salt and ground black pepper

Preheat the oven to 375°F.

Cut the eggplant in half lengthwise. Score the flesh and lightly brush the cut surface of each half with olive oil. Place the eggplant on a lightly oiled baking sheet, cut side down. Bake until very tender, about 35 minutes. The eggplant will look wrinkled and deflated. Remove it from the oven, and set aside to cool.

Heat the oil in a medium skillet. Add the onion and sauté for 3 to 5 minutes, until tender and translucent. Add the garlic and tomatoes and cook for 1 minute longer, stirring occasionally. Remove from the heat.

Scoop the flesh out of the eggplant halves and discard the skin. Chop the cooled eggplant into bite-size pieces and add it to the skillet with the tomato mixture. Add the basil, parsley, lemon juice, and sugar. Blend well. Salt and pepper to taste. Serve at room temperature.

Creamy Tofu Veggie Dip

Use this dip with fresh, sliced vegetables, such as carrots, cauliflower, broccoli, celery, and cherry tomatoes. It also makes a tasty dressing for a green leaf salad.

- 4 ounces soft silken tofu
- 2 tablespoons white miso
- 1 tablespoon finely chopped scallions
- 1 or 2 garlic cloves, minced
- 1½ tablespoons olive oil
- 1 tablespoon rice vinegar

Place all the ingredients in a blender, and process until smooth. If you don't have a blender, put the ingredients in a medium bowl and stir and whip with a wire whisk or fork. It won't be as smooth, but it will taste the same.

THREE

Sandwiches, Burgers, and Wraps

Cultures around the world have found unique ways to assemble entire meals into easy-to-eat packages. Check out Tex-Mex Tempeh Tacos (page 71), Greek Sandwiches with Tofu "Feta Cheese" (page 58), and the juicy Portobello Burger (page 65). The recipes offered here make convenient lunches or casual suppers.

Greek Sandwiches with Tofu "Feta Cheese"

PREPARATION TIME: 15 MINUTES
MAKES 2 SERVINGS

Marinate the tofu overnight and make the sandwich the next day. It's the perfect meal for eating outside in the sunshine.

2$\frac{1}{2}$ cups romaine lettuce, torn into bite-size pieces
$\frac{1}{4}$ small cucumber, peeled and thinly sliced (about $\frac{1}{3}$ cup)
1 small tomato, cored and chopped
$\frac{1}{4}$ cup chopped red onion
$\frac{1}{4}$ red bell pepper, diced (about $\frac{1}{3}$ cup)
$\frac{1}{2}$ cup Tofu Feta "Cheese" (recipe follows), cut into $\frac{1}{4}$-inch cubes
1$\frac{3}{4}$ teaspoons olive oil
1$\frac{1}{4}$ teaspoons fresh lemon juice
$\frac{1}{4}$ to $\frac{1}{2}$ teaspoon minced lemon zest*
Salt and ground black pepper
2 pitas, split in half to make 4 pockets
8 kalamata olives, cut in half

In a large bowl, toss the lettuce, cucumber, tomato, onion, bell pepper, and Tofu "Feta Cheese" with the olive oil. Add the lemon juice and lemon zest, and toss again. Salt and pepper to taste. Warm the pita halves in a dry skillet, then fill them with the salad and tuck in the olives.

*NOTE: Use a vegetable peeler or sharp knife to shave off the thin, bright yellow skin of the lemon, taking care not to peel off the bitter whitish tissue under the rind. If you are uncertain of the source of the fruit (whether it's organic or not), use hot water to remove whatever may have been sprayed on the surface.

Tofu "Feta Cheese"

PREPARATION TIME: 7 MINUTES
MARINATING TIME: OVERNIGHT
MAKES ABOUT $^1/_2$ CUP

The simple technique of bathing tofu in a brine solution captures the salty flavor of feta cheese. Parboiling the tofu first slightly firms its texture. It will keep for several days in the refrigerator.

    4 ounces firm tofu
    3 cups fresh water
    1 $^1/_2$ tablespoons salt
    1 $^1/_2$ teaspoons fresh lemon juice

Bring a small pot of water to a boil over high heat. Add the tofu and cook for 1 minute. Drain immediately. When the tofu is cool enough to handle, cut it into 3 pieces. In a small nonreactive bowl, place the fresh water, salt, and lemon juice. Stir well to dissolve the salt. Add the tofu (the bowl should have enough water to cover the tofu; add more water if necessary). Cover and marinate the tofu overnight in the refrigerator. Tofu feta will keep refrigerated for several days. When ready to use, remove from the brine and pat the tofu dry. Cut into small cubes.

Open-Faced Santa Fe Sandwiches with Tempeh

PREPARATION TIME: 20 MINUTES
MARINATING TIME: ABOUT 30 MINUTES
MAKES 2 SERVINGS

This hot tempeh sandwich boasts the flavors of a great Southwest barbecue.

$^3/_4$ cup Barbecue Sauce (page 181)
6 to 8 ounces multigrain tempeh
1 tablespoon vegetable oil
$^1/_2$ red bell pepper, cut into thin strips
1 cup chopped yellow onion (about $^1/_2$ medium onion)
1 whole-grain roll, split and toasted
2 tablespoons minced fresh parsley

Place the Barbecue Sauce in a medium bowl. Crumble the tempeh into the sauce and gently stir to coat. Marinate at room temperature for 30 minutes, stirring occasionally.

When the tempeh is ready, heat the oil in a medium skillet on medium heat. Add the bell pepper and onion and sauté for 5 minutes, or until the onion is tender and translucent, stirring constantly. Increase the heat to medium-high, add the tempeh, and sizzle for 30 seconds. Reduce the heat to low and cook, covered, for 3 minutes. Stir and cook, uncovered, on medium heat 4 minutes longer, stirring occasionally.

To assemble the sandwich, open the roll and toast each half on a lightly oiled skillet. Spoon the tempeh mixture on each of the bun halves, sprinkle with parsley, and serve.

Seitan Salad Sandwiches

PREPARATION TIME: 10 MINUTES
MAKES 2 SERVINGS

The sweetness of raisins and the crunchiness of apples and almonds combine with seitan to make an excellent take-along lunch.

4 ounces seitan (preferably the seasoned variety), diced
$^1/_4$ to $^1/_2$ of a small apple, cored and diced
$^1/_4$ teaspoon fresh lemon juice
1 small scallion, thinly sliced
1 tablespoon raisins
1 tablespoon slivered almonds
1 to 2 teaspoons minced fresh parsley
1 to 2 teaspoons sweet pickle relish
$^1/_3$ cup Tofu Wasabi Spread (page 127)*
1 pita, cut in half
Shredded romaine lettuce (about two lettuce leaves)

Place all the ingredients, except the lettuce and the pita, in a medium bowl. Gently stir to combine.

Warm the pita halves in a dry skillet for 20 to 30 seconds on each side. Spoon the filling into the pocket, and add the lettuce.

*NOTE: If you prefer, use a vegan mayonnaise dressing in place of the Tofu Wasabi Spread. Combine 1 tablespoon vegan mayonnaise, 2 teaspoons ketchup, and 1 teaspoon mustard.

Tempeh Reuben Sandwiches

PREPARATION TIME: ABOUT 15 MINUTES
COOKING TIME: ABOUT 30 MINUTES
MAKES 2 SERVINGS

Here tempeh is simmered in an apple juice marinade for about 30 minutes before assembling the sandwich. You can do this a day ahead, and then preparing the sandwich takes 5 minutes. Typically a Reuben sandwich is made with Swiss cheese; here cheese is replaced and outshined by the sweet flavor of slowly sautéed onions (the sautéed onions and tempeh keep well in the refrigerator for several days).

1 cup apple juice
2 tablespoons soy sauce
4 garlic cloves, chopped
3 slices fresh ginger ($1/8$- to $1/4$-inch-thick rounds)
6 ounces multigrain tempeh
1 tablespoon olive oil
$1/2$ medium yellow onion, sliced into rings
4 slices rye or whole-grain bread
$1/4$ cup sauerkraut, rinsed and drained
Vegan mayonnaise
Ketchup
Dijon mustard

Combine the apple juice, soy sauce, garlic, and ginger in a small saucepan. Add the tempeh, bring to a boil, immediately reduce the heat, and simmer, covered, for 30 minutes.

While the tempeh simmers, heat the olive oil in a small skillet over medium heat. Add the onions and sauté for 12 to 15 minutes, stirring occasionally, until the onions have turned golden brown. If sticking becomes a problem, add a little water.

To assemble the sandwiches, cut the tempeh into 2 pieces (each about $2\frac{1}{2}$ by 2 inches). Place 1 piece of cooked tempeh on a slice of bread, and top with half of the sauerkraut and onions. Spread mayonnaise, ketchup, and mustard on the second slice of bread, and put the sandwich together. Repeat the process when you're ready to make another sandwich.

Tofu-Basil Sandwiches

PREPARATION TIME: 30 TO 40 MINUTES
MAKES 2 SERVINGS

This tasty blend of tofu, basil, and tomatoes makes a good-looking sandwich. Serve it stuffed in a warm pita, and tuck in some mixed greens.

4 ounces firm tofu
1 tablespoon vegan mayonnaise
1 tablespoon ketchup
1 teaspoon fresh lemon juice
1/4 teaspoon minced garlic
1 teaspoon minced fresh basil
2 teaspoons chopped fresh parsley
2 tablespoons chopped toasted almonds*
1/2 cup chopped tomatoes
Salt and ground black pepper

Sandwich the tofu between two plates and rest a heavy book or weight on the top plate. Press for 20 to 30 minutes, then drain the expressed liquid from the plate.

Crumble the pressed tofu into a medium bowl. Add the mayonnaise, ketchup, lemon juice, and garlic. Stir and mash to combine. Stir in the basil, parsley, almonds, and tomatoes. Salt and pepper to taste.

*NOTE: Place the nuts in a small, dry skillet over medium heat. Stir the nuts or shake the pan constantly for 3 to 5 minutes, or until fragrant and lightly browned. Remove the nuts from the skillet immediately to stop the cooking process. Nuts can be toasted ahead of time and will keep in an airtight container for one to two weeks in the refrigerator, or for one to three months in the freezer.

Portobello Burger

PREPARATION TIME: 15 MINUTES
MAKES 1 SERVING

Slices of succulent portobello mushrooms and bell pepper strips served on a toasted whole-grain bun are good enough to make you want seconds.

1 tablespoon olive oil
1 garlic clove, minced
1 portobello, stem removed and cap cut into $1/2$-inch slices
$1/4$ small red or green bell pepper, cut into $1/4$-inch strips
Pinch of salt
1 teaspoon soy sauce
Pinch of sugar or natural sweetener
1 whole-grain bun
Dijon mustard
Vegan mayonnaise
Tomato slices
Red onion slices
1 or 2 lettuce leaves

Heat the oil in a medium skillet over medium heat. Add the garlic and sauté for 1 minute. Add the portobello, bell pepper strips, and salt; cook for about 5 minutes, stirring occasionally until the mushroom slices begin to soften. Add the soy sauce and sugar. Continue cooking and stirring 5 minutes longer, or until the mushroom slices are tender.

To assemble the burger, toast the bun and place it on a work surface. Spread the cut sides with mustard and vegan mayonnaise. Layer the mushroom mixture on one of the bun halves. Top with sliced tomato, onion, and lettuce. Put the bun together.

(continued)

NOTE: Cooked portobellos refrigerate well. If there are extras, you have a sandwich waiting.

VARIATION: For a Mexican version, wrap the mushrooms and peppers in a whole-wheat flour tortilla and warm in a microwave for 5 to 10 seconds. Top with salsa and cilantro.

Chipotle Chili-Black Bean Burgers with Sweet Corn Relish

PREPARATION TIME: 30 MINUTES
MAKES 3 BURGERS

These juicy burgers are sure to become one of your favorite meals.
Make the burgers as mild or as hot as you like.

$1^1/2$ tablespoons olive oil
$^1/2$ cup chopped red onion
2 garlic cloves, minced
$^1/4$ cup finely chopped carrot
$^1/4$ to $^1/2$ teaspoon chipotle chili powder*
$^1/2$ teaspoon ground cumin
One 15-ounce can black beans, rinsed and drained ($1^1/2$ cups
   cooked beans)
1 tablespoon Dijon mustard
1 tablespoon soy sauce
1 tablespoon ketchup
$^1/2$ cup rolled oats
Salt

Heat 2 teaspoons of the oil in a medium skillet over medium
heat. Add the onion and garlic and sauté for 3 to 5 minutes, until
the onions soften. Add the carrots, chipotle chili powder, and
cumin. Cook on low heat for about 5 minutes. Set aside.

Mash the beans in a large bowl with a potato masher or the
back of a large spoon (it takes a moment for the beans to give in,
but they will become creamy). Add the mustard, soy sauce,
ketchup, and sautéed vegetables. Stir in the oats, and salt to taste.

(continued)

Form the mixture into 3 burgers. Warm the remaining oil in the skillet and cook the burgers over medium-low heat for 5 to 6 minutes on each side. Serve immediately topped with Sweet Corn Relish (recipe follows), fresh salsa, or your choice of condiments.

*NOTE: If chipotle chili powder is unavailable, use ³/₄ teaspoon regular chili powder.

Sweet Corn Relish

PREPARATION TIME: 10 MINUTES
COOKING TIME: 20 MINUTES
MAKES 1 ¹/₂ CUPS

This fresh relish makes a good topping for bean dishes and for sandwiches, too.

³/₄ cup corn kernels
¹/₂ cup finely chopped tomato
¹/₂ cup finely chopped green bell pepper
¹/₂ cup finely chopped red onion
2¹/₂ tablespoons brown sugar or natural sweetener
¹/₂ cup cider vinegar
1 tablespoon Dijon mustard
1 garlic clove, minced

Bring all the ingredients to a boil in a saucepan over high heat. Reduce the heat to simmer, and continue cooking for 20 minutes. Store covered in the refrigerator. It will keep for 4 days.

Millet Patties with Zesty Tomato Relish

PREPARATION TIME: 25 MINUTES
COOKING TIME: ABOUT 30 MINUTES
MAKES 2 SERVINGS (EIGHT 3-INCH PATTIES)

Serve these eye-catching, colorful patties as a side dish or light meal, and top them Zesty Tomato Relish (recipe follows) or chunky salsa. Millet is a versatile, mild tasting grain that's worth adding to your cooking repertoire.

1/2 cup millet
2 cups hot water
1/8 teaspoon salt
1/2 teaspoon ground cumin
1/2 teaspoon dried thyme
1 1/2 tablespoons olive oil
1 small carrot, diced (about 1/4 cup)
1/4 cup diced onion
3 tablespoons toasted sunflower seeds*
1 tablespoon cornmeal
1/4 cup chopped fresh parsley
Salt and ground black pepper

In a dry, heavy-bottomed, 4-quart saucepan, toast the millet on medium-high heat, stirring constantly until it becomes fragrant, for 3 to 5 minutes (the millet will begin to pop and smell like popcorn). Carefully pour the hot water into the pot in a steady stream (heating the water before you add it to the pot reduces splattering). Bring the pot to a boil, reduce the heat to low. Add the salt, cumin, and thyme, cover, and cook for 25 to 30 minutes, or until the water is absorbed. When the millet is ready, remove the pot from the heat and set aside.

(continued)

In a medium skillet, heat $1/2$ tablespoon of the olive oil on medium heat. Add the chopped carrot and onion. Cook for 3 to 5 minutes, until the onion is soft and translucent.

Add the sautéed vegetables, sunflower seeds, cornmeal, and parsley to the millet. Stir to combine. Add salt and pepper to taste. When the millet is cool enough to handle, form the mixture into eight 3-inch patties.

Wipe out the skillet with a paper towel. Warm the remaining 1 tablespoon of olive oil in the skillet over medium-high heat. Add the patties and cook until each side is lightly browned. Serve hot.

*NOTE: In a small, dry skillet, toast the sunflower seeds on medium heat for 3 to 5 minutes, stirring frequently, until they become fragrant and begin to pop. Remove the seeds immediately from the skillet to stop the toasting process.

Zesty Tomato Relish

MAKES $1/2$ CUP

Prepare the relish while the millet cooks.

1 cup diced tomatoes
1 tablespoon fresh lemon juice
$1/4$ teaspoon ground cinnamon
1 garlic clove, minced
1 tablespoon raisins
$1/4$ teaspoon salt
$1/4$ teaspoon red pepper flakes
$1/2$ teaspoon sugar or natural sweetener

In a small saucepan combine all of the relish ingredients and simmer, covered, for 15 minutes.

Tex-Mex Tempeh Tacos

PREPARATION TIME: 15 MINUTES
MARINATING TIME: 30 MINUTES
MAKES 4 TACOS

Here tempeh is combined with the forceful flavors of Mexico to make dazzling tacos. For something extra, add chopped fresh cilantro, sliced scallions, pitted sliced black olives, or slices of avocado. Top it all with Tofu Sour Cream (page 125).

Marinade
- 3 tablespoons fresh lemon or lime juice
- 2 tablespoons salsa
- 2 tablespoons olive oil
- 1 tablespoon mild chili powder
- 1 teaspoon ground cumin
- Splash of Tabasco

- 6 ounces multigrain tempeh, cut into $1/4$- to $1/2$-inch cubes
- 4 regular-size (6-inch) corn or whole-wheat flour tortillas
- 1 small tomato, sliced
- 2 to 4 lettuce leaves, shredded

Add the marinade ingredients to a shallow bowl, and stir to combine.

Add the tempeh to the marinade and gently stir to coat the pieces. Marinate at room temperature for 30 minutes, turning the tempeh from time to time.

In a medium skillet on medium-high heat, sizzle tempeh for 30 seconds. Reduce the heat to low and cook, covered, for 3 minutes. Flip the tempeh and cook, uncovered, on medium heat for 3 to 4 more minutes, until the tempeh is browned. Set aside.

Heat the tortillas in a dry skillet until they are warm and pliable, and then fill them with the sizzled tempeh, tomato, lettuce, and your choice of extras. Serve immediately. Leftover, cooked tempeh will keep for several days in the refrigerator.

Indian Sweet Potato Wraps with Chutney

PREPARATION TIME: 25 MINUTES
MAKES 2 WRAPS

Chapati is a simple Indian flatbread made from flour and water, much like a Mexican flour tortilla. Top the wraps with store-bought chutney, or prepare Pear and Apple Chutney (page 117).

1 cup diced sweet potato (1/2-inch cubes)
4 teaspoons olive oil
1/2 cup chopped onions
1 garlic clove, minced
3 ounces soft silken tofu
1/8 teaspoon ground cinnamon
1 teaspoon fresh lemon juice
1/8 teaspoon salt
Dash of Tabasco or cayenne
1/4 cup frozen green peas, thawed
1/4 cup chopped fresh tomatoes
2 whole-wheat flour chapatis or flour tortillas (7-inch variety)
Chutney*

Preheat the oven to 425°F.

To a 4-quart saucepan, add the sweet potatoes and 2 teaspoons of the oil and stir to evenly coat the potatoes. Spread the potatoes in a single layer onto a baking sheet. Bake for about 15 to 20 minutes or until the potatoes are tender. Stir and turn the potatoes once or twice to ensure even cooking.

Warm the remaining two teaspoons of oil in the same saucepan, add the onions, and sauté on low for 10 minutes. Add the garlic and continue cooking for 5 minutes, stirring frequently. Remove from the heat and set aside.

When the sweet potatoes are ready, add them to the saucepan

with the onions and garlic. Add the tofu, cinnamon, lemon juice, salt, and Tabasco. Stir and mash with a fork until the mixture is creamy. Gently stir in the peas and tomatoes.

In a dry skillet, warm the chapatis or tortillas for 20 to 30 seconds on each side, until softened. Divide the potato filling in half. Place one portion of the filling in the center of a chapati and top with a generous spoonful of chutney. Fold the bottom edge of the chapati over the filling, and fold in both sides toward the center, leaving the top open to form a pocket. Repeat the process with the second chapati.

*NOTE: Chutney is best served warm or at room temperature.

Greens and Black Bean Quesadilla

PREPARATION TIME: 25 MINUTES
MAKES 4 SERVINGS

Tofu and greens combine to make a surprisingly creamy quesadilla without cheese. If you have extra quesadillas, store them in the refrigerator for a late-night snack or the next day's lunch. Top the quesadilla with a generous helping of salsa or serve with Pear and Apple Chutney (page 117).

Four 1/4-inch-thick slices firm tofu
2 teaspoons plus 1 tablespoon olive oil
1 to 2 teaspoons soy sauce
1 cup diced red onion
1 garlic clove, minced
1/2 teaspoon dried thyme
1/2 teaspoon ground allspice*
1/2 teaspoon salt
4 cups chopped greens (collard or kale)
1 tablespoon water
1/2 cup canned black beans, rinsed and drained
2 tablespoons orange juice
4 regular whole-wheat flour tortillas (6-inch)

Pat the tofu slices dry with a paper towel. Heat 2 teaspoons of oil in a medium skillet and sauté the tofu until it is lightly browned on both sides. Just before you remove the tofu from the skillet, add a splash of soy sauce, and sizzle the tofu for about 30 seconds, turning once. Remove the tofu from the skillet, and set aside.

Wipe the skillet clean with a paper towel, and use it to heat 1 tablespoon of oil on medium heat. Add the onion and garlic and sauté for 3 to 5 minutes, until the onions are translucent and tender. Add the thyme, allspice, and salt. Stir, then add the greens and water and sauté for 1 or 2 minutes, uncovered. Cover and cook until the greens are tender, about 5 to 8 minutes. If necessary, add more water.

When the greens are tender, push them to the side of the pan and add the beans and orange juice. Mash the beans with the back of a large wooden spoon or spatula, then stir everything together. Remove the skillet from the heat, and set aside.

Place the four tortillas on a flat surface. Spoon $1/4$ of the greens mixture on one half of each tortilla, and place a slice of tofu on top. Fold the tortilla over the filling.

Rewarm the skillet on medium heat. Transfer the quesadillas to the skillet, two at a time, and toast for 30 to 60 seconds on each side. Serve immediately.

*NOTE: Allspice is a berry that combines the flavors of several spices, including cloves, pepper, cinnamon, and nutmeg. You can buy it whole or ground.

Avocado and White Bean Burritos

PREPARATION TIME: 10 MINUTES
MAKES 2 SERVINGS

A recipe faster than this would be hard to find. The proportions for this filling are fairly arbitrary. If you like things hot, add more salsa or an extra shake of Tabasco. The arugula adds a peppery taste.

1/2 ripe Haas avocado (dark, knobby skin)
1 1/2 tablespoons fresh lemon juice
3/4 cup canned white or navy beans, rinsed and drained (about half of a 15-ounce can)
2 large whole-wheat flour tortillas (7 to 8 inches)
Store-bought salsa
Tabasco (optional)
2 to 4 tablespoons chopped fresh arugula or fresh cilantro

Cut the avocado in half. Use the half without the pit. Hold the avocado in the palm of your hand, pulp side up. Without piercing the skin, score the flesh in a crisscross pattern, and scoop the pulp into a medium bowl. Add the lemon juice and mash the avocado with the back of a large spoon or fork. Add the beans; mash the mixture some more, and stir to combine.

Warm the tortillas in a dry skillet for 20 to 30 seconds on each side. Spoon half of the avocado mixture onto each tortilla, and add the salsa. Sprinkle with Tabasco if you desire. Garnish with a generous amount of arugula. For something extra, you can also sprinkle on sliced scallions, black olives, or a few cherry tomatoes. Fold the bottom edge of the tortilla over the filling, and then fold in both sides toward the middle to create a pocket.

Temaki—Hand-Rolled Sushi

RICE COOKING TIME: ABOUT 45 MINUTES
PREPARATION TIME FOR ASSEMBLING HAND ROLLS: 10 MINUTES
MAKES 2 TO 4 SERVINGS

People wonder how vegans can enjoy sushi without fish. The answer is simple: vegans delight in the mixture of chewy seaweed, fresh sliced vegetables, sweet rice, and the nose-tingling rush of wasabi. Temaki are shaped like ice cream cones and are rolled in the palm of the hand. They make good snacks and great party food. Arrange a plate of sliced, fresh vegetables, prepare the rice and Wasabi Dressing (recipe follows), and let your guests assemble their own temaki. Serve with hot green tea.

1 cup water
½ cup short-grain brown rice
Pinch of salt
1 tablespoon seasoned rice vinegar, store-bought or homemade
  (recipe follows)
2 standard-size nori sheets (8 by 7 inches), cut in half
4 green lettuce leaves, trimmed to fit the roll
Wasabi Dressing (recipe follows)
2 carrots, thinly sliced
1 avocado, pitted, peeled, and thinly sliced

To a small saucepan, add the water, rice, and salt. Cover and bring to a boil over the highest heat. When steam escapes from below the lid, turn off the heat for 5 minutes (leave the pot on the burner). Return the burner to very low heat and simmer for about 40 to 45 minutes, or until the water is absorbed. Remove the pot from the heat and set aside, covered, for 10 minutes.

Place the warm rice in a large shallow wooden or glass bowl. Drizzle with seasoned rice vinegar. With a large spoon, fold the vinegar

(continued)

through the rice until the grains are coated. Don't overmix. Let the rice cool until it's comfortable to handle (if it's hot, it will wilt the nori).

Place a half sheet of nori in the palm of your hand, with the rough side facing up. Spread about $1/2$ cup of rice on half of the nori sheet. Set a small lettuce leaf on top of the rice (for an especially attractive presentation, place the lettuce on the nori so that it extends a bit above the top edge). Spread the Wasabi Dressing along the center of the lettuce in a line about $1/4$ inch wide (if you love wasabi, add more). Place the carrots and avocado in a line on top of the dressing.

Starting at the bottom corner of the rice, roll the nori over the filling toward the upper corner to form a cone. Serve with soy sauce and a dab of wasabi for dipping if you desire. Eat immediately.

Homemade Seasoned Rice Vinegar

1 tablespoon rice vinegar
1 to 2 tablespoons sugar or natural sweetener
Pinch of salt

Combine the ingredients in a small bowl and stir until the sugar is dissolved. Use about 1 tablespoon dressing for 1 cup of rice.

Wasabi Dressing

2 teaspoons wasabi powder
2 teaspoons water
2 tablespoons vegan mayonnaise

Combine the ingredients in a small bowl (make only as much as you plan to use immediately, because the flavor fades with time).

Other Filling Suggestions

Thinly sliced cucumber

Thinly sliced daikon radish

Thinly sliced scallions

Thinly sliced red peppers

Seasoned tofu

Cooked asparagus

Baby spinach leaves (fresh or lightly steamed)

Arugula

Fresh cilantro

Watercress

Toasted sesame seeds

FOUR

Soups and Quick Breads

There's something for everyone in a pot of soup, and it may be one of the world's oldest culinary brews. You begin most soups by sautéing onions and garlic for a few minutes and then tossing some chopped celery into the pot. After that it's up to you—there's a lot of room for improvisation in soup making. Add any other vegetables you have on hand with herbs and spices you like, and sauté until the vegetables are tender. Add the liquid: water, vegetable stock, canned tomatoes with their juice, or maybe some soy milk, and cook until everything is hot. It's that simple! For something extra, toss in some canned beans or cooked grains. It's easy to enjoy leftover soup, because the flavors mellow after the soup rests for a day or so in the refrigerator. Just reheat and eat. If you're too busy to turn on the stove, cold soup isn't bad either.

Most of the quick breads you'll find in this chapter are savory and pair well with many salads, stews, and soups.

Steadfast Winter Soup

PREPARATION TIME: 25 MINUTES
COOKING TIME: 35 TO 40 MINUTES
MAKES 4 SERVINGS

Here's an always-there-for-you soup that highlights rugged, earthy vegetables that deliver deep, sweet flavor.

1 tablespoon olive oil
$^1/_2$ medium yellow onion, chopped
$^1/_4$ small cabbage, cored and thinly sliced (about 2 cups)
2 medium carrots, thinly sliced
2 medium to large parsnips, peeled and thinly sliced
One 15-ounce can cannellini beans, drained and rinsed
2 garlic cloves, minced
1 small potato, such as Yukon Gold or red, diced
One 14.5-ounce can whole tomatoes with liquid, chopped*
2 cups water
1 teaspoon dried thyme
$^1/_2$ teaspoon salt
1 tablespoon balsamic vinegar
Pinch of sugar or natural sweetener
Ground black pepper
Chopped fresh parsley

Heat the oil in a 3- to 4-quart pot over medium heat. Add the onion, cover, and cook for 3 to 5 minutes, or until softened. Add the cabbage, carrots, and parsnips. Cover and continue cooking until the vegetables are soft, about 8 minutes, stirring occasionally.

Stir in the beans, garlic, potato, tomatoes, water, thyme, and salt. Increase the heat to medium-high, and bring the pot to a boil. Cover, and reduce the heat to low. Simmer for 20 to 30 minutes.

Remove from heat and stir in the balsamic vinegar and sugar. Salt and pepper to taste. Sprinkle with chopped parsley and serve.

*NOTE: Bypass the mess of chopping canned tomatoes on a cutting board and chop them while they're still in the can.

Spanish Tomato Soup

PREPARATION TIME: 25 MINUTES
MAKES 4 TO 6 SERVINGS

Lovely and uncomplicated, this chunky, rustic soup is great served with a crisp green salad.

- 2 tablespoons miso
- 2 tablespoons warm water
- 1 tablespoon olive oil
- $1/2$ medium onion, thinly sliced
- 3 large garlic cloves, minced
- 2 medium white or Yukon Gold potatoes, cut in quarters lengthwise, and thinly sliced
- $1/2$ teaspoon paprika
- 1 large tomato, chopped (about 1 cup)
- $1/2$ teaspoon dried thyme
- One 15-ounce can white beans, such as cannellini, navy, or kidney, drained and well rinsed
- $3^3/4$ cups water

In a small bowl, dissolve the miso in the warm water and set aside. In a 3- to 4-quart pot, heat the olive oil over medium heat, and sauté the onion, garlic, potatoes, and paprika, stirring constantly to keep the garlic from burning. Cook until the onions have softened, about 5 minutes. Add the tomatoes and thyme, and simmer for 3 to 4 minutes. Add the beans and the water, stirring to combine. Simmer gently for 10 minutes, or until the potatoes are tender. Serve hot.

Rice Noodles with Shiitake-Ginger Broth

PREPARATION TIME: 15 MINUTES
MAKES 2 SERVINGS

Don't let the escargot look of the mushrooms frighten you; they add interesting flavor. This soup is so much better than the freeze-dried ramen noodle soups sold in supermarkets. It's a meal worthy of slurping.

4 ounces thin rice noodles or angel hair pasta
1 teaspoon sesame oil
4 cups kale, tightly packed
3 1/2 cups water
1 carrot, finely sliced
4 freeze-dried shiitake mushrooms*
1 cup black beans, drained
2 teaspoons finely minced fresh ginger
3 tablespoons brown rice miso, dissolved in 1/2 cup hot water

Cook the rice noodles in a pot of boiling water for 5 to 7 minutes, until just tender, or cook according to package directions. Thin noodles cook quickly, so keep an eye on the pot to avoid overcooking. Drain the noodles, splash with the sesame oil, stir, and set aside.

While the noodles cook, wash the kale. Slice the leaves off the stems, discard the stems, and chop the leaves into bite-size pieces. Set aside.

Put the water in a large pot, and add the carrot and mushrooms. Bring the pot to a boil, then reduce the heat to medium, cover, and cook for 5 minutes. Add the kale, beans, and ginger. Don't worry if the pot seems full; the kale will wilt. Continue to cook, uncovered, at a rolling boil until the kale is tender, about 5 minutes.

(continued)

When the kale is ready, turn off the heat and stir in the miso and noodles. Ladle into deep bowls. Sprinkle with Asian hot sauce if you like, and serve immediately.

*NOTE: Freeze-dried shiitake mushrooms do not need presoaking for this recipe. If they are unavailable, use regular dried shiitakes. Soak regular dried shiitakes in $1/3$ cup hot water for 5 to 10 minutes to soften. Remove the stems and discard. Add the soaking liquid to the soup.

Red Lentil and Beet Soup

PREPARATION TIME: 15 MINUTES
COOKING TIME: 30 MINUTES
MAKES 5 SERVINGS

Red lentils are small and salmon-colored, and when cooked they become soft and creamy, making them ideal for soups. The cider vinegar, added at the end, provides a bright-tasting finish.

One 15-ounce can sliced beets
1 tablespoon olive oil
$1/2$ medium onion, chopped (about $3/4$ cup)
1 medium carrot, sliced
1 cup red lentils, washed and drained
6 cups water
1 teaspoon salt
2 tablespoons apple cider vinegar
Tofu Sour Cream (page 125)
1 to 2 tablespoons chopped fresh parsley or fresh cilantro (optional)

Drain and discard the liquid from the can of beets. Cut the beets into small bite-size pieces with a knife while they are inside the can.

Heat the oil in a 3- to 4-quart pot and sauté the onion until it is soft and translucent. Add the carrot and sauté another minute. Add the beets, lentils, water, and salt.

Bring to a boil. Reduce the heat and simmer, uncovered, for 30 minutes. Remove from heat and stir in the vinegar. Serve topped with Tofu Sour Cream, and sprinkle on chopped cilantro or parsley, if desired.

Quinoa and Butternut Squash Soup

PREPARATION TIME: 15 MINUTES
MAKES 4 SERVINGS

Bright golden squash and luminous quinoa harmonize to make an attractive, rich-tasting soup. Slices of warm corn bread are all you need for a complete meal.

    1 tablespoon olive oil
    1 medium onion, finely chopped
    2 cups seeded, peeled, and diced butternut squash*
    1/4 cup quinoa, well rinsed (page 153)
    2 garlic cloves, minced
    3 cups vegetable stock
    Salt and ground black pepper
    Tabasco (optional)
    Chopped fresh parsley or fresh cilantro

Heat the oil over medium heat in a 3- to 4-quart pot. Add the onion and sauté for 5 minutes, until translucent. Add the squash, quinoa, and garlic, and sauté for another 5 minutes. Add the stock, and salt and pepper to taste. Bring to a boil, cover, reduce the heat, and simmer for 15 minutes, or until the squash is tender. Remove from the heat.

Use a potato masher to lightly mash the squash. Taste. If necessary, add salt and pepper. Serve sprinkled with chopped parsley or cilantro, and a splash of Tabasco sauce, if desired.

*NOTE: To peel butternut squash, cut it in half lengthwise and scoop out the seeds. Set it cut side down on a cutting board and peel each half before cutting it into chunks or dicing it.

Green Split Pea Soup
with Seitan

PREPARATION TIME: 15 MINUTES
COOKING TIME: 50 TO 60 MINUTES
MAKES 4 SERVINGS

It takes only minutes to mix up this good-for-you soup, and then it cooks for about an hour. It's worth the wait.

- 1 1/2 cups green split peas
- 1 tablespoon olive oil
- 1 medium onion, chopped (about 1 cup)
- 2 medium carrots, sliced
- 1 cup diced seitan (preferably seasoned variety)
- 8 cups water
- 1/2 to 3/4 teaspoon salt
- 1/4 teaspoon red pepper flakes
- 1 teaspoon fresh, or 1/2 teaspoon dried, rosemary
- Minced scallions or Rustic Garlic Croutons (page 123)

Pour the split peas onto a plate and run your fingers through the pile to remove any stones or debris. Place the peas in a colander and rinse. Set aside.

Warm the oil in a 3- to 4-quart pot over medium heat. Add the onions and sauté for 3 to 5 minutes, until soft and translucent. Add the carrots and seitan, and sauté another minute, stirring constantly. Add the water, peas, salt, and red pepper flakes. Bring to a boil, then lower heat and gently boil, partially covered (this allows steam to escape and the liquid to reduce, which deepens the flavor). Stir occasionally.

Cook for 50 to 60 minutes, until the peas are tender. Fifteen minutes before the soup is ready, add the rosemary. Ladle into serving bowls, and top with minced scallions or Rustic Garlic Croutons.

Yellow Split Pea Soup with Sweet Potatoes and Carrots

PREPARATION TIME: 20 MINUTES
COOKING TIME: 50 TO 60 MINUTES
MAKES 2 SERVINGS

Mellow-tasting yellow split peas are punctuated with salsa for an economical, comforting meal.

1 tablespoon oil
$1/3$ cup finely chopped onion
2 garlic cloves, minced (about 2 teaspoons)
1 heaping teaspoon minced fresh ginger
$1/2$ teaspoon ground cumin
$1/2$ teaspoon chili powder
$1/2$ cup peeled and diced sweet potato
1 small carrot, sliced (about $1/3$ cup)
4 cups vegetable broth or water
$1/4$ cup medium-hot salsa
$1/2$ cup yellow split peas
$1/4$ teaspoon salt
1 tablespoon fresh lime juice
$1/4$ cup frozen green peas or sliced scallions*

Warm the oil in a 3- to 4-quart pot over medium heat. Add the onion, garlic, and ginger. Sauté, stirring frequently, until the onion is soft, about 2 minutes. Stir in the cumin, chili, sweet potato, and carrot. Add the broth, salsa, split peas, and salt. Stir briefly, scraping the bottom of the pot to make sure all of the spices are mixed into the liquid.

Cover, and bring to a boil. Reduce the heat and continue cooking, covered, at a gentle boil. Cook for 50 to 60 minutes, stirring occasionally, until the split peas are soft and have lost their shape.

Stir the lime juice into the soup, and ladle into serving bowls. Serve garnished with green peas or sliced scallions.

*NOTE: Just before serving, bring 1 cup of water to a boil in a small saucepan. Add the peas and cook briefly, about 1 minute. Drain (avoid overcooking the peas or they'll lose their bright green color).

Creamy Portobello Mushroom Soup

PREPARATION TIME: 25 MINUTES
MAKES 3 SERVINGS

Tender carrots, celery, and onions combine with portobello morsels and float in a velvety broth.

1 1/2 tablespoons olive oil
1/2 medium onion, diced (about 1/2 cup)
1 garlic clove, minced
1 carrot, thinly sliced (about 1/2 cup)
1 celery stalk, diced
1 portobello mushroom, chopped (about 4 ounces)
1/4 teaspoon salt
1 teaspoon dried marjoram
2 cups vegetable broth
2 tablespoons flour
2 cups soy milk
2 teaspoons soy sauce
1/8 to 1/4 teaspoon cayenne pepper
Chopped fresh parsley

Warm the oil in 3- to 4-quart pot over medium heat. Add the onion, garlic, carrot, celery, portobello, salt, and marjoram. Sauté for 10 minutes, stirring frequently.

Put 1/4 cup of the vegetable broth into a 1-cup container. Add the flour and stir well to make a smooth paste. Set aside.

Add the remaining 1 3/4 cups vegetable broth, soy milk, soy sauce, and cayenne to the pot. Bring the pot to a boil. Slowly pour the flour mixture into the soup, stirring constantly. As soon as the flour mixture is added, reduce the heat and simmer for 10 minutes, stirring occasionally.

Ladle the soup into bowls, and garnish with chopped parsley.

Chilean Two-Potato Soup

PREPARATION TIME: 15 MINUTES
COOKING TIME: 35 MINUTES
MAKES 4 SERVINGS

You'll be surprised how quickly this hearty soup is simmering on the stove. Preparation requires cutting only four ingredients and opening a few cans.

1 tablespoon olive oil
$1/2$ cup minced onion
2 garlic cloves, minced (about 2 teaspoons)
1 cup diced sweet potato
1 medium red or yellow potato, cut into a $1/2$-inch dice
One 4-ounce can green chilies
One 15-ounce can red kidney beans, drained (about $11/2$ cups)
1 cup corn kernels
4 cups vegetable broth
$1/2$ teaspoon dried thyme
$1/2$ teaspoon ground cumin
$1/8$ teaspoon cayenne
$1/4$ teaspoon salt
Fresh lemon or lime juice
Minced fresh parsley

Warm oil in a 3- to 4-quart pot over medium heat. Add the onion and garlic and sauté for 3 to 5 minutes, until the onion is soft. Add the potatoes, chilies, beans, corn, broth, thyme, cumin, cayenne, and salt. Stir, bring to a boil, and then reduce heat to a gentle boil and cook uncovered for 30 minutes.

Ladle the soup into bowls, add a squeeze of lemon or lime juice, and garnish with minced parsley.

Pumpkin Scones

These colossal golden scones are irresistible spread with fruit preserves and accompanied by a cup of strong coffee. They do well alongside a bowl of hot chili, too.

1 cup all-purpose flour
$1/2$ cup whole-wheat flour
$1/2$ cup cornmeal
2 teaspoons baking powder
$1/4$ teaspoon salt
$1/2$ cup dried cranberries*
6 ounces canned pumpkin ($3/4$ cup)
$3/4$ cup soy milk
$1/4$ cup vegetable oil
$1/4$ cup pure maple syrup

Preheat the oven to 450°F. Lightly oil a baking sheet.

To a large bowl, add the flours, cornmeal, baking powder, and salt. Whisk or stir well to distribute the baking powder and salt throughout the mixture. Add the dried cranberries and stir again. Set aside.

In a medium bowl, combine the pumpkin, soy milk, oil, and maple syrup. Add the pumpkin mixture to the flour mixture, stirring just to combine. Do not overmix or the scones will be tough. Drop the batter by $1/4$ cups onto the baking sheet, 1 inch apart.

Bake for 12 to 15 minutes, until lightly browned on top. Serve hot.

*NOTE: If cranberries are unavailable, substitute raisins.

Quinoa Corn Bread

PREPARATION TIME: 10 MINUTES
BAKING TIME: 25 TO 30 MINUTES
MAKES 6 GENEROUS SERVINGS

In this recipe, corn bread gets a protein and calcium boost with quinoa. To give corn bread a lovely, golden undercrust, heat the baking pan or skillet in the oven until it's hot before adding the batter.

1¼ cups yellow cornmeal
1 cup unbleached all-purpose flour
2½ teaspoons baking powder
1 teaspoon salt
1 cup corn kernels
1 cup soy milk or other nondairy milk
3 to 4 tablespoons pure maple syrup
1 cup cooked quinoa (page 153)*
¼ cup canola oil

Preheat the oven to 400°F. Generously oil a 6 × 10-inch baking dish or a medium cast-iron skillet.

To a large bowl, add the cornmeal, flour, baking powder, and salt and stir to combine.

In a small saucepan, heat the corn and drain.

To a medium bowl, add the soy milk, maple syrup, corn kernels, quinoa, and canola oil. Pour the wet ingredients into the dry flour mixture, and stir with a few quick strokes just until a batter forms. Transfer the batter to the hot baking pan or hot skillet. Bake for 25 to 30 minutes, until a toothpick inserted into the center comes out clean.

*NOTE: This corn bread can be made without the quinoa and is delicious either way.

Rustic Olive Rolls

PREPARATION TIME: 15 MINUTES
BAKING TIME: ABOUT 12 MINUTES
MAKES 10 LARGE BISCUITS

These fragrant rolls are studded with black olives, onions, and a hint of sage. The thick batter goes right from mixing to baking, eliminating rolling dough.

1 cup whole-wheat flour
1 cup unbleached all-purpose flour
2 teaspoons baking powder
1/4 teaspoon salt
2 teaspoons crumbled, dried sage leaves
1/4 cup pitted kalamata olives
1/2 cup onions, finely chopped
1/3 cup canola oil
1 cup plus 2 tablespoons soy milk

Preheat oven to 450°F. Lightly oil a baking sheet.

To a large bowl, add the flours, baking powder, salt, and sage. Mix well with a fork or wire whisk to combine. Cut the olives into fourths. Stir the olives and onions into the flour mixture.

In a separate bowl, combine the oil and soy milk. Pour the liquid into the flour mixture, then stir just to combine. The batter will be thick; avoid overmixing, which results in tough rolls.

Drop the batter by 1/4 cups onto the baking sheet 1 to 2 inches apart. Bake for about 12 minutes, until the rolls are lightly browned. Serve hot.

Three-Grain Molasses Bread with Walnuts and Raisins

PREPARATION TIME: 15 MINUTES
BAKING TIME: 40 TO 45 MINUTES
MAKES 1 LOAF

Unsulfured blackstrap molasses is extremely high in iron and calcium. The bread is slightly sweet and makes a great toast for breakfast.

1 1/2 cups soy milk
2 tablespoons fresh lemon juice
1 1/2 cups unbleached all-purpose flour
1 cup whole-wheat flour
1/2 cup cornmeal
1/4 cup brown sugar or natural sweetener
2 teaspoons baking soda
1/2 teaspoon salt
1/2 cup chopped walnuts
1/2 cup raisins
1 teaspoon lemon zest*
1/2 cup unsulfured blackstrap molasses**

Preheat the oven to 350°F. Lightly oil a 9 × 5-inch loaf pan.

Pour the soy milk into a small bowl. Add the lemon juice and set aside for 5 minutes to give bubbles a chance to form.

In a large bowl, stir together the all-purpose flour, whole wheat flour, cornmeal, brown sugar, baking soda, salt, walnuts, raisins, and lemon zest.

Add the soy milk mixture and molasses to the flour mixture and stir just to combine. Pour the batter into the loaf pan and bake for

(continued)

40 to 45 minutes, until the loaf is firm and a knife or toothpick inserted into the center comes out clean. Cool the bread in the pan for 15 minutes, then remove from the pan, slice, and serve warm. Let the bread cool completely before wrapping for storage.

*NOTE: Use a vegetable peeler or sharp knife to shave off the thin, bright yellow skin of the lemon, taking care not to peel off the bitter whitish tissue under the rind. If you are uncertain of the source of the fruit (whether it's organic or not), use hot water to remove whatever may have been sprayed on the surface.

**NOTE: Before you measure the molasses, lightly oil the measuring cup, and the molasses will slide out easily.

FIVE

Salads

Salads can be cool, juicy, crunchy, and even warm. You'll find them all represented here.

Baby Spinach Salad with Apples

PREPARATION TIME: 10 MINUTES
MAKES 2 SERVINGS

Most green salads are noteworthy for their crispness. This one is unique because it's warm and wilted. Choose a good eating apple, such as Gala, Fuji, or Golden Delicious, for slicing. Almost every supermarket has bags or bins of prewashed and dried spinach leaves, which makes this recipe especially easy to prepare.

2 tablespoons fresh lemon juice
1 to 2 teaspoons pure maple syrup
$\frac{1}{4}$ teaspoon ground cumin
$\frac{1}{4}$ teaspoon minced fresh ginger
$\frac{1}{8}$ teaspoon salt
$\frac{1}{2}$ apple, cored and cut lengthwise into thin pieces
4 loosely packed cups baby spinach leaves, washed and dried*
2 tablespoons olive oil
2 tablespoons toasted almonds, chopped**

In a small bowl, stir together the lemon juice, maple syrup, cumin, ginger, and salt. Add the sliced apple and stir to coat. Set aside.

Put the spinach in a large bowl. Heat the olive oil in a medium skillet until nearly smoking. Pour the oil over the spinach and toss quickly. If the spinach is not wilted to your taste, transfer it to the hot skillet and press and stir, so that it wilts but does not cook, about 1 to 2 minutes.

Transfer the spinach back to the large bowl, add the apple mixture, and toss. Sprinkle with toasted almonds, and serve.

*NOTE: If you're not using prewashed and dried spinach, prepare the leaves by floating them in a large bowl of water, and let the sand and grit sink to the bottom. Remove the leaves and dry thoroughly.

**NOTE: Place the nuts in a small, dry skillet over medium heat. Stir the nuts or shake the pan constantly for 2 to 3 minutes, until the nuts are fragrant and lightly browned. Remove the nuts from the skillet immediately to stop the cooking process. Nuts can be toasted ahead of time and will keep in an airtight container for one to two weeks in the refrigerator, or for one to three months in the freezer.

Jicama and Orange Salad

Jicama (hic-a-ma) is a large root vegetable with a crunchy texture and sweet, nutty taste similar to an apple. It looks ugly on the outside, but under its thin skin is a sweet surprise. Look for a jicama about the size of a grapefruit. For a quick snack, sprinkle slices of jicama with lime juice and chili powder, or use slices as chips, and dip them in salsa. This salad makes a refreshing side dish for tacos or bean burritos.

$1/2$ cup jicama, peeled and cut into matchsticks
1 medium orange, peeled and cut into bite-size pieces (about 1 cup)
$1/2$ teaspoon fresh lemon juice or fresh lime juice
$1/2$ teaspoon olive oil
$1/8$ teaspoon salt
Pinch of sugar or natural sweetener
Dash of ground black pepper
Dash of chili powder
Fresh cilantro leaves or chopped fresh parsley

Put the jicama and orange pieces in a medium bowl. Sprinkle with the lemon juice, olive oil, salt, sugar, pepper, chili powder, and cilantro, and stir to combine. Taste. If you like a sweeter taste, sprinkle on more sugar. If you like a hotter taste, add more chili or pepper.

Serve in a small bowl or on a lettuce leaf. Store any leftovers in a covered bowl in the refrigerator. This salad tastes good the next day.

Mango Slaw with Sesame Vinaigrette

PREPARATION TIME: 15 MINUTES

MAKES 4 SERVINGS

This lively slaw uses delicate, ruffled napa cabbage. If you like slaw with volume and loft, add the dressing just before serving.

  4 cups finely chopped napa cabbage
  1/2 cup finely chopped carrot
  1/4 cup chopped scallions
  1/8 teaspoon salt
  1 small mango, cut into bite-size pieces (about 1 cup)*
  1/2 cup toasted almonds, chopped**

  To a large bowl, add the cabbage, carrot, scallions, salt, and mango. Add the chopped almonds and vinaigrette (recipe follows). Toss and serve.

Sesame Vinaigrette

PREPARATION TIME: 7 MINUTES

MAKES 1/2 CUP

This bright dressing is also good on green leaf salads.

  2 tablespoons orange juice
  1 tablespoon rice vinegar
  1 tablespoon pure maple syrup
  1/2 tablespoon minced fresh ginger
  2 1/2 tablespoons canola oil

(continued)

1 tablespoon toasted sesame oil
$^1/_2$ teaspoon salt
Dash of ground black pepper

Put all the ingredients in a small jar and shake well, or add the ingredients to a small bowl and whip with a fork.

*NOTE: For how to select and cut a mango, see page 115.

**NOTE: Toast almonds on a dry baking sheet in a preheated 350°F. oven for 5 minutes, or until fragrant and lightly browned. Remove immediately from the pan to stop the cooking process.

Chipotle Slaw

PREPARATION TIME: 10 MINUTES
MAKES ABOUT 4 SERVINGS

This snappy slaw is made with chipotle chilies, which are dried smoked jalapeños prepared in a spicy chili puree. It's hot stuff, so use it carefully. Remember, you can always add more—there are many chilies in a small can or jar. To save the extras for future use, place them, individually, on a plate or tray and freeze, then put the pieces in an airtight container and store in the freezer. Add chipotle chilies to soups, mashed potatoes, salad dressing, corn bread, and bean dishes when you want a powerful, smoky flavor.

$^1/_3$ cup vegan mayonnaise
$1^1/_2$ tablespoons fresh lemon or fresh lime juice
$^1/_4$ teaspoon ground cumin
$^1/_2$ teaspoon chipotle chilies in adobo sauce, minced
4 cups finely chopped cabbage*
$^1/_2$ cup chopped jicama or red bell pepper
2 tablespoons chopped fresh cilantro
Salt

To a large bowl, add the vegan mayonnaise, lemon juice, cumin, and chilies. Stir to combine. Add the cabbage, jicama, and cilantro. Stir to coat the vegetables. Salt to taste and serve.

*NOTE: Standard tricolor slaw mix with carrots, green cabbage, and purple cabbage is a good choice for this salad.

Fruited Slaw with Sunflower Seeds

Using precut salad mix makes this fruited slaw speedy to prepare. For something extra, toss in sliced peeled pears, or diced apples.

- 1 tablespoon olive oil
- 2 tablespoons fresh lemon juice
- 1 to 2 teaspoons pure maple syrup
- 3 cups cabbage, thinly sliced, or precut classic green slaw mix with carrots
- 1 to 2 oranges, peeled, seeded, and chopped
- $1/2$ cup raisins
- $1/4$ cup toasted sunflower seeds*
- Salt

Pour into a medium bowl the olive oil, lemon juice, and maple syrup. Add the cabbage, oranges, raisins, and toasted sunflower seeds. Toss gently to coat well. Salt to taste. Serve right away, or cover and store in the refrigerator. The slaw will keep for 2 to 3 days.

*NOTE: In a small, dry skillet, toast the sunflower seeds on medium heat for 3 to 5 minutes, stirring frequently, until they become fragrant and begin to pop. Remove the seeds immediately from the skillet to stop the toasting process.

Fattoush Bread Salad
with Hummus

PREPARATION TIME: 25 MINUTES
MAKES 2 SERVINGS

Many Mediterranean countries have their own bread salad. This Lebanese version, not surprisingly, is made with toasted pita bread.

1 whole-wheat pita (6-inch variety)
$1/2$ medium cucumber, peeled, seeded, and chopped* (about $1/2$ cup)
1 medium tomato, chopped
$1/4$ small green bell pepper, chopped (about $1/4$ cup)
1 to 2 scallions, thinly sliced
$1/4$ cup chopped fresh parsley
$1/4$ cup chopped fresh mint
1 cup shredded romaine lettuce
Dressing (recipe follows)
$1/2$ cup hummus, store-bought or homemade (recipe follows)

Preheat the oven to 350°F.

Place the pita on a baking sheet and bake until lightly toasted, turning once or twice, 10 to 15 minutes.

To a medium bowl, add the cucumber, tomato, bell pepper, scallions, parsley, and mint. Break or tear the toasted pita into bite-size pieces, and add them to the salad. Add 2 tablespoons dressing, and gently toss to coat the salad.

Stack the lettuce leaves and roll them up like a sleeping bag. Slice the roll into ribbons of green. Arrange the greens on two serving plates and spoon the cucumber mixture on top. Garnish each serving with a generous scoop of hummus. Drizzle with extra dressing if you like, and serve.

(continued)

*NOTE: To seed a cucumber, cut the cucumber in half lengthwise, and with the tip of a spoon, scrape out the seeds.

Dressing

1 or 2 garlic cloves, minced
2^1/$_2$ tablespoons fresh lemon juice
2^1/$_2$ tablespoons olive oil
^{1}/$_4$ teaspoon salt
^{1}/$_4$ teaspoon ground cumin

Add all the ingredients to a small bowl. Whip with a fork or wire whisk to combine.

Hummus

PREPARATION TIME: 10 MINUTES
MAKES 2 CUPS

Hummus invites adaptation. If you like fresh lemon juice, add more. If you love garlic, add an extra clove. Store hummus in a covered container in the refrigerator. It will keep for 5 days.

One 15-ounce can garbanzo beans
2 teaspoons lemon zest*
2 tablespoons lemon juice
1 or 2 cloves garlic
1 tablespoon roasted tahini (sesame seed butter)
Salt and ground black pepper

Drain the garbanzo beans over a bowl to collect the liquid; reserve the liquid. To a food processor or blender, add the garbanzo beans, lemon zest, lemon juice, garlic, and roasted tahini. Whirl until smooth. Salt and pepper to taste. If the mixture is too stiff, add 1 to 2 more teaspoons lemon juice or some of the reserved can liquid. The hummus should be soft but stiff enough to hold its shape.

*NOTE: Use a vegetable peeler or sharp knife to shave off the thin, bright yellow skin of the lemon, taking care not to peel off the bitter whitish tissue under the rind. If you are uncertain of the source of the fruit (whether it's organic or not), use hot water to remove whatever may have been sprayed on the surface.

VARIATION: To turn this Middle Eastern hummus into a Greek version for spreading on crusty bread, or to use as a dip with fresh vegetables, omit the tahini and add a splash of olive oil instead. For hummus with a rosy glow, add some chopped roasted red pepper. You can also change the flavor with a dash of cayenne, cumin, fresh parsley, or cilantro. This dish is perfect for experimentation, so be adventurous! You can easily make this recipe your own by trying out your favorite spices and add-ins.

Millet Salad with Curry-Ginger Dressing

PREPARATION TIME: 15 MINUTES
COOKING TIME: 25 TO 30 MINUTES
MAKES 3 SERVINGS

Millet has been a staple grain to many world cultures for thousands of years. It's popular in this country as a seed sold to feed small birds. Unlike the millet found in pet stores, the millet you buy in natural food markets is hulled and ready to cook. It has a mild-tasting, nutty flavor and is a rich source of B vitamins.

1/2 cup millet*
1 1/2 cups hot water
1/8 teaspoon salt
1/4 cup canned garbanzo beans, drained and rinsed
1 small carrot, finely chopped (about 1/4 cup)
1/2 medium red bell pepper, chopped (about 1/2 cup)
2 tablespoons raisins
5 to 6 tablespoons Curry-Ginger Dressing (recipe follows)
Lettuce (about 1 cup per serving)
Fresh chopped cilantro
Chopped dry-roasted, unsalted peanuts

In a dry, 4-quart saucepan, toast the millet on medium heat for 3 to 5 minutes, stirring constantly, until it becomes fragrant (the millet will begin to pop and smell like popcorn).

Carefully pour the water into the pot in a steady stream (heating the water before you add it to the pot reduces sputtering). Add the salt and bring the pot to a boil. Reduce the heat to low and stir. Cover and cook for 25 to 30 minutes. Set aside to cool for a few minutes.

Fluff the millet with a fork. Add the garbanzo beans, carrot, red bell pepper, and raisins. Drizzle with Curry-Ginger Dressing and toss to coat the grain. Taste. Add more dressing if necessary.

Roll the lettuce leaves into a cigar shape and slice into ribbons of green, or tear the lettuce into small bite-size pieces. Arrange the lettuce on plates and add the millet. Garnish with cilantro and peanuts, and serve.

*NOTE: If water is left in the pot once the millet is tender, drain the water, and transfer the millet to a large bowl. If there is no water left in the pot, and the millet is still crunchy after cooking, add 1 to 2 tablespoons of hot water, and continue cooking, covered, until the millet is tender, about 4 to 5 minutes.

Curry-Ginger Dressing

PREPARATION TIME: 10 MINUTES
MAKES $^1/_2$ CUP

This distinctive dressing can also be used on steamed vegetables and cooked rice.

2 tablespoons rice vinegar
$^1/_4$ cup canola oil
1 tablespoon mellow brown rice miso
$^1/_2$ to $^3/_4$ teaspoon curry powder
$^1/_4$ to $^1/_2$ teaspoon minced fresh ginger
1 small garlic clove, minced
1 teaspoon brown sugar or natural sweetener
1 tablespoon warm water

Combine ingredients in a small bowl and stir to dissolve the miso and sugar. The dressing will keep in the refrigerator, covered, for a week.

Mixed Greens with Figs

Figs have been a delicacy for thousands of years. They are packed with calcium, potassium, iron, and fiber. Add chopped figs to hot oatmeal and green leaf or grain salads. Sprinkle them on mashed sweet potatoes or baked squash. Figs make good snacks sliced in half and studded with walnuts or almonds.

$\frac{1}{4}$ to $\frac{1}{2}$ teaspoon minced orange zest*
1 tablespoon fresh orange juice
$\frac{1}{4}$ tablespoon rice vinegar
$1\frac{1}{2}$ tablespoons olive oil
Pinch of salt
4 cups mixed greens, washed and torn into bite-size pieces
6 dried Black Mission or Calimyrna figs, stems removed and quartered
1 orange, peeled and sliced into bite-size pieces
$\frac{1}{4}$ cup toasted walnuts, chopped**

To a large bowl, add the orange zest, orange juice, vinegar, olive oil, and salt. Whisk with a fork or wire whisk to combine. Add the greens to the bowl and toss to coat. Place the greens on two serving plates. Scatter the figs, orange pieces, and nuts on top of each salad. Serve at once.

*NOTE: Zest is the thin bright outer skin of the citrus fruit without the white undercoat. Use a vegetable peeler or sharp knife to shave off the zest, taking care not to peel off the bitter whitish tissue under the rind. If you are uncertain of the source of the fruit (whether it's organic or not), use hot water to remove whatever may have been sprayed on the surface.

NOTE: Toast the nuts on an unoiled baking sheet in a preheated 350°F. oven for 3 to 5 minutes, or until fragrant and lightly browned. Remove immediately from the sheet to stop the cooking process. When the nuts are cool, chop and set aside. Nuts can be toasted ahead of time and will keep in an airtight container for one to two weeks, or for one to three months in the freezer.

Quinoa Tabouli

Here is a variation on the traditional Middle Eastern salad usually made with bulghur or cracked wheat. This version uses cooked quinoa. Whichever grain you use, it's always refreshing. For something extra, add toasted sunflower seeds, kalamata olives, pieces of baked tofu, or sizzled tempeh.

4 tablespoons olive oil
2 tablespoons fresh lemon juice
2 garlic cloves, finely minced
2 cups cooked quinoa (page 153)
$^3/_4$ cup finely chopped fresh parsley
2 scallions, finely sliced
2 medium tomatoes, finely chopped (about 1$^1/_2$ cups)
Salt and ground black pepper
Romaine or red lettuce leaves, cut into $^1/_4$-inch ribbons (about
    1$^1/_2$ cups per serving)

In a medium bowl, mix together all of the ingredients except the lettuce. Salt and pepper to taste. Place ribbons of lettuce on each plate, and top with the salad, then serve.

Carrot Salad with Chutney and Peanuts

PREPARATION TIME: 10 MINUTES
MAKES 1 TO 2 SERVINGS

If your meal already includes plenty of greenery, consider this as a side dish. Here chutney adds a new twist to timeless carrot salad.

1 tablespoon natural-style peanut butter
1 tablespoon hot water
$1/4$ teaspoon fresh lemon juice (optional)
Pinch of salt (optional)
1 cup finely chopped carrots (about 3 medium carrots)
1 to 2 tablespoons Pear and Apple Chutney (page 117) or store-bought chutney
1 tablespoon dry-roasted, unsalted peanuts or chopped almonds
Minced fresh parsley or fresh cilantro

In a small bowl, combine the peanut butter, hot water, and lemon juice, if using, to make a thick, smooth sauce. Add more water if necessary. Taste. Add salt if needed, and set aside.

In a medium bowl, combine the carrots, chutney, and peanuts. Add the peanut butter mixture, and stir to coat. Serve sprinkled with parsley or cilantro.

Tropical Fruit Medley

PREPARATION TIME: 10 MINUTES
MAKES 4 TO 5 CUPS

Cut fruit ready and waiting is irresistible. Simple combinations of fresh fruit can double as dessert or a refreshing salad. In this recipe, the cook wins the prize—the white mango seed. There's always a bit of mango left on the stone after you slice off the pulp. Peel off any remaining skin, and pull the seed through your teeth like an artichoke leaf or edamame pod and enjoy the pleasantly fibrous texture of the pit.

¾ cup reduced-fat (light) coconut milk
3 tablespoons orange juice
2 teaspoons sugar or natural sweetener (optional)
1½ cups bite-size pieces of fresh pineapple
1 mango, sliced (about 1 cup)
1 to 2 tablespoons minced fresh mint leaves (optional)
1½ cups canned mandarin oranges, drained

How to Select and Slice a Pineapple

A pineapple worth eating should smell fragrant, have bright, crisp top leaves, and feel heavy for its size. Pass on fruits with soft spots.

To cut a pineapple, start by cutting off the leafy crown. Using a large, heavy knife, halve the fruit lengthwise from bottom to top, then cut the two halves in half again to form quarters. Slice out the section of core from the top of each wedge-shaped quarter, then slide a knife between the flesh and rind to free the flesh.

How to Select and Cut a Mango

Only one mango variety, the Keitt, is still green when ripe; when it's soft to the touch, it's sweet, juicy, and ready to eat. All other mangoes should have started to color when you buy them, or they may never ripen.

Mangoes have a large pit, so you can't cut a mango in half. Slice the mango cheeks from end to end along the broad, flat side of the pit. Peel the cheeks like an apple; then cut the flesh into pieces. Or, for a spectacular presentation and a mango that looks like a porcupine, score the flesh in each cheek into a grid, taking care not to pierce the skin. Hold the scored mango in your hand, and bend the skin backward, turning it "inside out," so the cubes pop up. Slice the cubes away from the skin. Peel and slice any fruit left on the pit.

In a medium bowl, combine the coconut milk, orange juice, and sugar. Stir in the pineapple, mango, and mint, add the mandarin oranges, and gently stir to avoid breaking the orange segments. Serve immediately.

SIX

Toppings

Toppings are a sure way to draw the flavors of a dish together. Most of the recipes in this chapter take only 5 to 10 minutes to prepare, yet are so flavorful that you'll find yourself making them again and again.

Pear and Apple Chutney

Most supermarkets stock chutney, but when you have the time, it's easy and less expensive to make your own blend, and it tastes better than most store-bought brands. This chutney will keep refrigerated for two weeks and is a tasty topping for steamed vegetables or warm rice. It smells wonderful as it's cooking. Chutney is traditionally served at room temperature.

1 large, ripe pear, cored and coarsely chopped
1 apple, cored and coarsely chopped
^{1}/$_4$ cup minced onions
2 tablespoons raisins
^{1}/$_4$ cup brown sugar or natural sweetener
^{1}/$_4$ cup rice vinegar
^{1}/$_4$ teaspoon ground cinnamon
^{1}/$_2$ teaspoon minced fresh ginger

In this recipe, it's unnecessary to peel the pear and apple. Combine all the ingredients in a medium saucepan, and bring to a boil. Reduce the heat to medium-low and cook for 25 to 30 minutes, uncovered, stirring occasionally, until the fruit and onions are soft and the liquid is syrupy.

Gomasio—Sesame Salt

Gomasio is a striking Japanese condiment made from toasted sesame seeds and sea salt. Use it in place of salt, sprinkled on sautéed vegetables, salads, grains, beans, rice, potatoes—anywhere you'd like a distinctive, salty flavor. It's great stuff!

  7 tablespoons sesame seeds
  1 tablespoon sea salt

Place the sesame seeds and salt in a dry skillet over medium heat, stirring constantly to keep the seeds from burning. Watch closely, as they can burn surprisingly fast. Toast for 4 to 5 minutes, until the seeds are fragrant and lightly browned. Immediately remove the mixture from the skillet to stop the seeds from browning.

Grind the seeds and salt with a mortar and pestle, suribachi (ridged Japanese bowl with wooden pestle), pepper mill, or small plastic hand grinder that fits in the palm of your hand. You'll find these grinders in Asian food markets for about $3. It is a simple tool that does a perfect job. Use it like a pepper mill to grind only what you need for your meal. You can also grind gomasio in an electric coffee grinder, food processor, or blender.

Whatever grinding method you select, the result should be cracked seeds, not a powder or sesame butter. Store the mixture in a tightly sealed container in the refrigerator. It will keep for several weeks.

NOTE: The ratio of sesame seeds and salt in this recipe is 7 to 1. Adjust the proportions to your liking. Buy untoasted sesame seeds and toast them as needed.

Shallot and Mushroom Gravy

Who doesn't smile when they see a bowl of gravy? It's lovely poured over sautéed tempeh or seitan, and everyone knows it's fantastic on mashed potatoes or biscuits.

- 4 shallots, thinly sliced (about ¾ cup)*
- 3 tablespoons olive oil
- 4 ounces cremini mushrooms, thinly sliced (about 2 cups)
- Pinch of salt
- 2 tablespoons unbleached all-purpose flour
- 2 cups soy milk
- ¼ teaspoon ground black pepper

In a medium saucepan on medium heat, sauté the shallots in the olive oil for 3 to 5 minutes, until they are translucent and slightly browned. Add the mushrooms and a pinch of salt. Sauté 1 to 2 minutes, then sprinkle on the flour and stir until it is absorbed, about 1 minute. Slowly stir in the soy milk and pepper. Simmer for 2 to 3 minutes, until slightly thickened. Serve hot.

*NOTE: If shallots are unavailable, substitute ½ cup finely chopped yellow onion.

Marinara Sauce

When a store-bought tomato sauce won't do, cook up this classic tomato sauce to use on all types of pasta, grains, and pizza. It's easy to make and keeps refrigerated for a week or frozen for a month. Vary the flavor with additions of sautéed mushrooms, capers, or black olives.

   3 tablespoons olive oil
   1 onion, chopped
   3 large garlic cloves, minced
   One 28-ounce can whole tomatoes, with their juice
   3 tablespoons chopped fresh basil
   ^{1}/$_2$ teaspoon dried oregano
   2 teaspoons dried rosemary, crumbled
   Salt and ground black pepper

   In a large skillet, warm the olive oil over medium-high heat and sauté the onion for 3 minutes. Add the garlic and sauté 3 minutes longer. Lower the heat to medium-low. Add the liquid from the tomatoes, and coarsely chop the tomatoes with a knife right in the can. Stir in the tomatoes, basil, oregano, and rosemary. Gently simmer for 20 minutes, stirring occasionally. Remove from the heat and let cool. Salt and pepper to taste.

Spanish Hazelnut-Red Pepper Sauce

PREPARATION TIME: 15 MINUTES

MAKES 3 CUPS

Use this versatile sauce like gravy and spoon it on steamed vegetables, cooked grains, or hot potatoes. Serve it over pasta or as a dip for fresh vegetables. Spread it on crackers or toasted chunks of artisan bread. If hazelnuts are not available, toasted almonds will work. You'll need a blender or food processor for this recipe.

$1/2$ cup whole hazelnuts
$1^1/2$ tablespoons olive oil
1 red bell pepper, chopped (about 1 cup)
2 medium fresh tomatoes, chopped
2 garlic cloves, chopped
$1^1/2$ teaspoons red wine vinegar
$1/8$ teaspoon cayenne
3 ounces soft silken tofu
Salt

Preheat oven to 325°F. Spread the nuts on an unoiled baking sheet and toast for 8 to 10 minutes, or until the nuts are fragrant. Immediately transfer the nuts to a plate to cool.

Blender Tip

Always cool a mixture before adding it to a blender. High heat and the closed lid can cause the pressure in the blender to rise and possibly blow the lid off the appliance.

(continued)

Warm the olive oil in a saucepan on medium heat. Add the bell pepper, tomatoes, garlic, vinegar, and cayenne. Cook on high to medium-high for 5 minutes, stirring occasionally. Remove from the heat and cool slightly. Transfer the mixture to a blender. Add the toasted nuts and tofu. Process until smooth. Salt to taste.

Rustic Garlic Croutons

PREPARATION TIME: 5 MINUTES
BAKING TIME: ABOUT 25 MINUTES
MAKES 4 CUPS

Homemade croutons have much better flavor and texture than the dry, rock-hard varieties you buy at the supermarket. Add croutons to crisp green salads or sprinkle them on top of a bowl of hot soup. They freeze well but taste so good that you may find they disappear before you can stash them in the freezer.

4 slices whole-grain bread, cut into $1/2$-inch cubes
2 tablespoons olive oil
1 large garlic clove, minced
$1/8$ teaspoon salt
1 tablespoon finely minced fresh parsley

Preheat the oven to 300°F.

Put all the ingredients into a bowl and toss well. Spread on an unoiled baking sheet and bake for 15 minutes. Turn the croutons with a spatula and bake another 10 minutes, until nicely browned.

Italian-Flavored Tempeh Nuggets

PREPARATION TIME: 15 MINUTES
MAKES ³/₄ CUP

Toss marinated tempeh nuggets into salads, cooked vegetables, or grain dishes. They're also good finger food for snacking.

3 to 4 ounces multigrain tempeh

Marinade
1 tablespoon olive oil
1¹/₂ teaspoons balsamic vinegar
1¹/₂ teaspoons soy sauce
1 garlic clove, minced
¹/₄ teaspoon red pepper flakes
¹/₂ teaspoon dried thyme leaves
¹/₂ teaspoon dried rosemary leaves

Cut the tempeh into ¹/₂-inch-wide cubes. Combine the marinade ingredients in a lidded container. Add the tempeh, and move the pieces around in the marinade to coat. Cover, and refrigerate for an hour or overnight. The tempeh will quickly absorb all of the marinade.

Heat a medium skillet over medium-low heat. Add the tempeh, cover, and cook for about 10 minutes, turning the pieces with a spatula occasionally, until they are lightly browned.

Serve immediately, or store in a covered container in the refrigerator and use before the expiration date on the tempeh package.

Tofu Sour Cream

PREPARATION TIME: 5 MINUTES
MAKES $^1/_3$ CUP

Tofu sour cream is a perfect topping option for tacos, baked potatoes, and many soups.

    3 ounces soft silken tofu
    2 teaspoons olive oil
    1 $^1/_2$ teaspoons rice vinegar
    1 $^1/_2$ teaspoons fresh lemon juice
    Pinch of salt

In a bowl with deep sides, combine all the ingredients with a fork or wire whisk, mashing the tofu against the sides and whipping until it's creamy. It will keep refrigerated for 2 to 3 days.

Fresh Basil Pesto

PREPARATION TIME: 10 MINUTES
MAKES ¹/₂ CUP

Use this pesto on pasta, pizza, and baked potatoes. It also makes a lively sandwich spread, and can be used as a flavoring for soups, stews, and tofu scrambles. A blender or food processor is necessary for this recipe.

1 garlic clove, peeled
3 tablespoons toasted walnuts or almonds*
¹/₄ teaspoon salt
1 cup loosely packed fresh basil
2 tablespoons olive oil

Combine all the ingredients in a blender or food processor and process until the pesto becomes a paste.

*NOTE: Place the nuts in a small, dry skillet over medium heat. Stir the nuts or shake the pan constantly for 3 to 4 minutes, until the nuts are fragrant and lightly browned. Remove the nuts from the skillet immediately to stop the cooking process. Nuts can be toasted ahead of time and will keep in an airtight container for 1 to 2 weeks in the refrigerator, or for 1 to 3 months in the freezer.

Tofu Wasabi Spread

PREPARATION TIME: 3 MINUTES
MAKES ⅓ CUP

Use this flavorful spread in place of mayonnaise on a sandwich or as a topping for a baked potato.

3 tablespoons soft silken tofu
2 teaspoons ketchup
1 teaspoon Dijon mustard
½ teaspoon wasabi powder

Place all the ingredients in a small bowl and whip with a fork or wire whisk to combine. Taste. If you like your food hot, add more wasabi.

Gremolata

Gremolata is a classic Italian condiment that combines parsley and lemon zest. Sprinkle it on various vegetables, grains, pastas, soups, and bean dishes. For a variation on this classic condiment, mince a small basil leaf or fresh rosemary with the gremolata, or add orange zest to the mix.

> Zest from 1 medium lemon*
> 1 or 2 garlic cloves
> ⅓ cup fresh parsley leaves

Place the lemon zest, garlic, and parsley on a cutting board and finely chop them together.

*NOTE: Use a vegetable peeler or sharp knife to shave off the thin, bright yellow skin of the lemon, taking care not to peel off the bitter whitish tissue under the rind. If you are uncertain of the source of the fruit (whether it's organic or not), use hot water to remove whatever may have been sprayed on the surface.

SEVEN

Vegetables

In a vegan diet, vegetables reign supreme. It's easy to make a satisfying meal with a heaping plate of steamed, roasted, or sautéed fresh vegetables adorned with nothing more than a squeeze of lemon and a dash of salt and ground black pepper. In this chapter you'll find new ways to prepare old favorites, along with ideas for making some less common vegetables.

Twice-Baked Potato Stuffed with Broccoli

PREPARATION TIME: 15 MINUTES
COOKING TIME: 60 MINUTES
MAKES 1 SERVING

Baked potatoes beat microwaved potatoes any day, not in the time they take to cook, but in their flavor and texture. People who have grown up eating microwaved potatoes may disagree, but many would argue that the crispy skin and the steaming dry-moist inside of an oven-baked potato is worth the wait. Bake two potatoes instead of one, and you'll have a head start on another meal.

A baked russet potato can become a meal in itself topped with chili or chunky tomato salsa. For a dessert-type potato, top a baked sweet potato with fragrant chutney.

1 russet or sweet potato*
2 teaspoons olive oil
1 large garlic clove, minced
1/8 teaspoon red pepper flakes
1/4 bunch broccoli, finely chopped (about 1 cup)
1/4 cup water
Salt

Preheat the oven to 400°F.

Wash the potato and pierce the skin in one or two places with a knife to allow steam to escape. Bake for 50 to 60 minutes, or until the inside is soft. Test for doneness by gently squeezing the middle of the potato (use a pot holder). If it gives in easily to your touch, it's done. Remove the potatoes from the oven, and lower the oven temperature to 350°F.

To a medium saucepan, add the oil, garlic, and red pepper flakes. Sauté for 1 minute on medium heat. Add the broccoli and stir for 30 seconds. Add the water, cover, reduce the heat, and simmer for 10 minutes, or until the broccoli is tender.

When the potato is cool enough to handle, cut it in half lengthwise. Scoop out the inner part, leaving $\frac{1}{4}$ inch of the potato on the skin to strengthen the shell. Add the pulp to the broccoli, blending with a fork until combined. Salt to taste. Refill the potato shells with the mixture. Place the stuffed potato halves on a baking sheet and drizzle with a small amount of olive oil. Bake for 15 to 20 minutes.

*NOTE: When you select a russet potato, make sure that the skin has an even brown tone. Avoid potatoes with a greenish case, because they're bitter. The potato should feel firm with no gouges, splits, or eyes.

Batter-Fried Cauliflower Pakoras

PREPARATION TIME: 15 MINUTES
MAKES 1 SERVING

If you've had a less than passionate relationship with cauliflower, this recipe will turn it into a love affair. These crispy morsels will melt in your mouth. You can batter-fry almost any vegetable in this manner—broccoli especially makes a good alternative. Brew up a pot of hot tea and serve the pakoras with ketchup or a generous spoonful of chutney for dipping.

> About 2 cups cauliflower florets, sliced into cross sections no more than $1/2$ inch thick.

Batter
$1/2$ cup unbleached all-purpose flour
1 teaspoon curry powder
$1/2$ teaspoon salt
$1/2$ teaspoon baking powder*
$1/3$ cup water
Canola oil for frying

To a large bowl, combine the flour, curry powder, salt, baking powder, and water to make a smooth, thick batter. It should not be runny. If necessary, add more water 1 to 2 tablespoons at a time. Mix well.

Warm $1/2$ inch of oil in a medium skillet on medium heat. The oil is ready for frying when a drop of batter quickly crisps. Coat the cauliflower slices in the batter, and carefully place them in the pan to avoid splashing the hot oil. Don't crowd the pan. Cook until golden on both sides, turning once, for 2 to 3 minutes on each side. Transfer to a paper towel to drain. Serve as soon as possible.

*NOTE: Make sure to check the expiration date on the baking powder.

Fast Vegetable Sautés

Knowing how to sauté enables you to create countless dishes without a recipe, and almost all vegetables can be sautéed.

Some vegetables take longer to cook than others, so cut those that take longer smaller and they will cook faster, or add them to the pan first to give them a head start. The middle of the pan may be hotter than the edges, so stir often.

Avoid overfilling the pan. Excessive food will drop the heat and cause the items to steam, not brown. It is far better to sauté your food in batches than to crowd the pan and produce limp food.

Many recipes begin with aromatic items such as chopped garlic or ginger. This helps infuse the following ingredients with their flavor. Watch the heat, since these delicate aromatics can burn by the time you are done sautéing the remaining ingredients.

Go for the Green with Kale, Collards, and Chard

Greens are a great source of calcium. The large leaves of some varieties may look formidable in the supermarket, but when cooked they shrink into a velvety mound, so you'll need to use more than you might imagine. Greens pair well with mild-flavored cooked grains such as rice, polenta, and noodles. They harmonize with creamy mashed potatoes, and add color and texture to soups and stir-fries.

Greens take only minutes to prepare. Choose one of the following cooking methods, and check out these great topping ideas:

- Toss cooked greens with toasted sesame oil, toasted sesame seeds, and a splash of soy sauce.

- Dress with a blast of lemon juice or balsamic vinegar and olive oil.

- For a sweet, irresistible taste, sprinkle cooked greens with raisins and chopped nuts.

- Add a few pinches of Gomasio (page 118).

- Toss with Gremolata (page 128).

- Serve with chutney.

- Sprinkle greens with corn-bread croutons.

The Stems

Chard: Cut 1 to 2 inches off the bottom of the stems, discard, and use the rest.

Collards and Kale: Slice the leaves off the stems, and discard the entire stem.

The Leaves

Stack chard or collard leaves. Roll them up like a sleeping bag, and slice through all the leaves at once to make ribbons of green. Roughly chop kale.

Basic Blanched Greens

4 cups water
Pinch of salt
$1/2$ to 1 bunch chard, collards, or kale, rinsed and sliced (about
  4 cups)

In a medium saucepan, bring the water to a boil with the salt. Add the greens and cook for about 2 minutes, or until the leaves are tender. Drain well in a colander. Shake and bounce the colander to get rid of excess water, then press the greens with the back of a large spoon to squeeze out the rest. Serve hot.

Sautéed Greens

PREPARATION TIME: 3 TO 7 MINUTES
MAKES 1 TO 2 SERVINGS

$1/2$ to 1 bunch chard, collards, or kale, rinsed and sliced (about
    4 cups)
1 tablespoon olive oil
1 garlic clove, thinly sliced

Wash the leaves and do not dry them. The water that clings to
the leaves will help the greens cook. In a large pan, warm the oil
over medium-high heat. Add the garlic and sauté for 1 minute,
stirring frequently. Add the greens and sauté for another 3 to 5
minutes, until wilted but still vibrantly green. If necessary, add a few
teaspoons of water to help steam the greens. Serve hot.

Green Beans
with Mustard Dressing

French, Asian, and Italian flavors combine to make a vibrant side dish to accompany a hearty sandwich, a steaming baked potato, or sautéed tofu.

4 cups water
1/2 pound stemmed green beans, fresh or frozen (about 2 cups)
1 tablespoon olive oil
1 teaspoon Dijon mustard
1/4 teaspoon dried oregano
Salt and ground black pepper
1 tablespoon toasted sesame seeds*

Bring the water to a boil in a medium saucepan. Add the beans and cook, uncovered, for 2 to 3 minutes, so that the beans are still bright green and crisp. Drain. Warm the oil in a medium skillet over medium heat. Add the beans and sauté for 2 to 3 minutes, until crisp-tender, stirring occasionally.

Combine the mustard and oregano in a large bowl. Add the beans and toss with the dressing, stirring to coat. Add salt and pepper to taste. Sprinkle with the sesame seeds and serve immediately.

*NOTE: In a small, dry skillet, toast the sesame seeds over medium heat for 3 to 4 minutes, stirring or shaking the pan constantly until the seeds are lightly browned. Immediately remove the seeds from the skillet to stop the cooking process.

Roasted Root Vegetables with Garlic Butter

PREPARATION TIME: 10 MINUTES
COOKING TIME: 35 TO 45 MINUTES
MAKES 2 SERVINGS

Roasting vegetables rather than boiling them caramelizes their natural sugars and intensifies their sweetness. Rinse the vegetables, chop them into chunks, toss them with dressing, and pop them into the oven. It's that simple! Leftover roasted vegetables make tasty additions to cooked grains or soups.

In this recipe garlic heads are tucked into the corner of the pan to make garlic butter. The garlic turns soft and creamy and is lovely spread on slices of crusty bread. Heat a little olive oil in a skillet, add slices of bread, and toast on both sides until golden. Remove the bread from the skillet, squeeze the garlic paste from the cloves, and spread it onto the bread like butter. Sealed and refrigerated, roasted garlic will keep for at least a week.

Balsamic-Olive Oil Dressing

2 tablespoons olive oil
1 tablespoon balsamic vinegar
$1/2$ teaspoon dried thyme leaves
$1/2$ teaspoon dried rosemary
$1/2$ teaspoon salt
$1/8$ teaspoon ground black pepper

In a large bowl, whisk together the dressing ingredients, and set aside.

Vegetables

   1 or 2 garlic heads

   2 small beets or 1 medium beet, peeled and cut into 1-inch
      chunks (about 1 cup)

   1 small sweet potato, peeled and cut into 1-inch chunks (about
      1 cup)

   2 medium carrots, cut into 1-inch chunks

   2 medium parsnips, peeled and cut into $^1/_2$-inch-thick slices

   1 small onion, cut into wedges

   Olive oil

Preheat oven to 425°F.

Remove as much of the outer papery skin from the garlic head as you can without breaking apart the cloves. Trim off the top $^1/_4$ inch, and set the garlic aside.

Add the beets, sweet potato, carrots, parsnips, and onion to the Balsamic–Olive Oil Dressing and toss well to evenly coat the vegetables. Spread in a single layer in an oiled baking pan. Don't crowd the pan or the vegetables will steam, not roast. If necessary, use two pans. Place the garlic in the corner of the pan, and drizzle it with olive oil.

Bake for about 45 minutes, stirring every 20 minutes, until the vegetables are crispy and tender.

Almost all vegetables can be roasted: zucchini, bell peppers, potatoes, tomatoes, squash, eggplant, and asparagus, to name a few. To roast hard and soft vegetables together, preheat the oven to 425°F. Cut the vegetables into bite-size pieces, oil a baking pan, and roast the hard vegetables for 15 minutes. Remove the pan from the oven. Add the soft vegetables and sprinkle on Balsamic–Olive Oil Dressing or drizzle generously with olive oil and a pinch of salt and pepper. Stir to coat the vegetables. Bake for about 30 minutes, stirring occasionally, until lightly browned and tender.

Seasoned Oven-Fries

Use a large potato because a small one will leave you wishing for more.

1 russet potato
1 teaspoon olive oil
1 teaspoon paprika
$1/4$ teaspoon ground cumin
Salt

Preheat the oven to 425°F.

Wash the potato well and peel if you wish. Cut the potato in half lengthwise. Then cut each half into $1/2$-inch-thick slices. Stack the slices, and cut into $1/2$-inch-wide strips.

Combine the oil, paprika, and cumin in a large bowl. Add the potatoes and stir to evenly coat.

Arrange the potato slices in a single layer on a lightly oiled baking sheet. Bake on the middle shelf of the oven for 20 to 30 minutes, or until the fries are golden and crisp. If you desire, serve sprinkled with fresh lemon juice and salt to taste, or add a side of ketchup for dipping.

Coconut-Flavored Creamed Corn

PREPARATION TIME: 10 MINUTES
MAKES 2 SERVINGS

Serve this fragrant vegetable dish with warm red lentils, a baked sweet potato, sautéed seitan, or sizzled tempeh.

1 tablespoon olive oil
1/2 cup diced onion
1 teaspoon curry powder
1 1/2 cups corn kernels
3/4 cup light unsweetened coconut milk
1 teaspoon fresh lime juice
Salt and ground black pepper

In a small saucepan, warm the oil on medium heat. Add the onion and sauté for 3 to 5 minutes, until soft and translucent.

Add the curry powder and stir well. Continue to cook, stirring frequently, for 1 minute. Curry powder burns easily, so keep an eye on the pot.

Stir in the corn, cover, and cook for 2 minutes. Stir in the coconut milk and heat thoroughly, but do not simmer or boil. Remove from the heat. Add the lime juice, salt and pepper to taste, and serve.

Maple-Flavored Brussels Sprouts with Carrots and Toasted Pecans

PREPARATION TIME: 10 MINUTES
MAKES 1 TO 2 SERVINGS

Do you like Brussels sprouts? If your answer is yes, you're probably in the minority. Yet their dubious reputation may be due only to what people don't know about them. For instance, it's important to choose fresh, young Brussels sprouts, and they're not always easy to find. Shop for them with your nose. Avoid old ones with a strong odor. Look for small, compact heads with bright green color and pass up any that are large and puffy-looking. If you've never tried eating Brussels sprouts and are feeling adventurous, test out this recipe and you'll discover a crunchy new vegetable.

1 cup Brussels sprouts (about 5)
Pinch of salt
1 small carrot, cut into ¼-inch rounds
1 to 2 teaspoons olive oil
Pinch of ground black pepper
1 teaspoon pure maple syrup
1 tablespoon finely chopped toasted pecans*

Trim off the root end of the Brussels sprouts, and discard any discolored outer leaves. Cut the sprouts in half. Bring a saucepan of water to a boil, and add the sprouts with a pinch of salt. Cook for 3 minutes. Add the carrot rounds and cook another 3 to 4 minutes, until the Brussels sprouts are crisp-tender. The Brussels sprouts should be bright green when you remove the vegetables from the water. Drain and rinse under cold water to stop the cooking process. This keeps the sprouts from turning pale green.

In a small skillet, warm the oil on medium heat. Add the Brussels sprouts, carrots, and a pinch of salt and pepper. Sauté for 2 to 3 minutes, until the vegetables are warm. Transfer to a bowl, drizzle with the maple syrup, and stir to coat. Serve sprinkled with the toasted pecans.

*NOTE: Place the nuts in a small, dry skillet over medium heat. Stir the nuts or shake the pan constantly for 2 to 3 minutes, until the nuts are fragrant and lightly browned. Remove the nuts from the skillet immediately to stop the cooking process. Nuts can be toasted ahead of time and will keep in an airtight container for 1 to 2 weeks in the refrigerator, or for 1 to 3 months in the freezer.

EIGHT

Basic Beans and Grains

Basic Beans

Beans have been feeding people all over the world for thousands of years. They are a vitamin-packed source of protein in a vegan diet, high in fiber and low in fat. Beans can be added to practically anything. Toss them into soups, sautés, and salads. They also make great dips and sandwiches. For convenience, the recipes in this book use canned beans; you can substitute home-cooked beans if you like. Canned beans are usually high in salt, so drain and rinse the beans before adding them to a recipe.

Cooking Dried Beans

Most people in the United States don't eat dried beans because they don't know how to cook them. When you're ready to cook a pot of beans from scratch, here's how to do it. It's simple!

1. Sort through the beans to get rid of any small stones or debris, and rinse them to remove any dust.

2. Soak the beans overnight or during the day in a big bowl covered with a generous amount of cold water. The water level should rise above the beans by 2 to 3 inches. Soaking beans rehydrates them and shortens the cooking time. It also helps begin breaking down some of the complex sugars in beans that cause digestive gas in some people. Thorough cooking dissolves more of the sugars (people vary in their reactions to foods, so don't assume that what is "gassy" for someone else will be "gassy" for you).

3. To cook the beans, drain the soaking water and transfer the beans to a pot. Add enough fresh water to cover the beans by 2 inches. The amount of water depends on the size of your pot. Simmer the beans, covered, on low heat, stirring occasionally. Make sure there's enough water in the pot to cover the beans at all times while they cook. Add salt or acidic foods, such as tomatoes, when the beans are tender. Adding them before will toughen the beans and lengthen the cooking time.

Beans Get Interesting

Turn a bean pot into a stew pot by stirring in chopped vegetables for the last half hour of cooking.

Add a splash of vinegar or lemon juice to cooked beans. You'll be amazed at the sparkle it adds to the pot.

Experiment with different combinations of herbs and spices. A pot of kidney or pinto beans can become a tasty chili when you add chopped onion, green pepper, garlic, chili powder, and ground cumin.

Cook white beans with a chopped carrot, onion, and celery rib. Add a pinch of oregano. When the beans are tender, stir in 2 tablespoons of olive oil, salt, and a dash of cayenne pepper.

Stovetop Cooking Guide for Soaked Beans

Generally 1 cup of beans yields about 2 to $2^{1}/_{2}$ cups of cooked beans. The cooking time will vary depending on the type and age of the bean.

BEANS (1 CUP DRIED)	WATER (CUPS)	COOKING TIME
Adzuki	3	50 minutes
Anasazi	$3^{1}/_{2}$	$1^{1}/_{2}$ hours
Black	$3^{1}/_{2}$	$1^{1}/_{2}$ to 2 hours
Black-eyed pea	3	1 hour
Cannellini	$3^{1}/_{2}$	$1^{1}/_{2}$ to 2 hours
Chickpeas (garbanzo)	4	3 hours
Great Northern	$3^{1}/_{2}$	$1^{1}/_{2}$ to 2 hours
Kidney	$3^{1}/_{2}$	2 hours
Lentils*	3	35 to 45 minutes
Navy	$3^{1}/_{2}$	$1^{1}/_{2}$ to 2 hours
Pinto	$3^{1}/_{2}$	2 hours
Split peas*	3	45 minutes

*Lentils and split peas do not require presoaking.

Cooking Grains

Throughout history most cultures have relied on grains as the foundation of their meals, and they are an integral part of vegan cooking. Because of their mild flavor, grains can be used in everything from soup to desserts. Grains have a delightful chewiness and add great texture to meals. Here are some of the most popular grains you'll find in a vegan kitchen.

Rice

Rice is grown on every continent except Antarctica. There are hundreds of varieties ranging in color from black to white. Short-grain rice is moister than long-grain rice and is better for sushi and desserts. Long-grain rice is good when you want a slightly dry, fluffy rice. You can substitute aromatic whole-grain basmati or jasmine rice in most recipes that use long-grain brown rice.

Once you've cooked rice, there are endless possibilities for quick meals. Cooked rice will keep in an airtight container in the refrigerator for up to three days.

Reheating Cooked Rice

To reheat cooked rice in a microwave, place 1 cup of rice in a microwavable container with 2 tablespoons of water. Cover and microwave on high for 1 minute.

To reheat cooked rice on the stovetop, place 1 cup of rice in a small saucepan with 2 tablespoons of water. Cover and cook on medium heat for 3 to 4 minutes, until most or all of the water is absorbed.

Whole-Grain Brown Rice

A good pot with a tight-fitting lid is best for cooking rice, because it keeps excessive steam from escaping, and the rice is less likely to burn. Avoid stirring the rice while it cooks or it may become gummy.

1 cup brown rice
2 cups fresh water
Pinch of salt

Put the rice into a 4-quart pot. Rinse the rice to remove any debris, and drain. Add the water and salt. Cover the pot and bring to a boil on high heat. Keep an eye on the pot. As soon as steam escapes from beneath the lid, turn off the heat for 5 minutes. Return to very low heat and simmer for 40 to 45 minutes, or until the rice is tender and the water has been absorbed. Remove the pot from the heat and allow the finished rice to sit, covered, for 5 minutes before serving.

Polenta

Polenta is a simple cornmeal pudding that makes a fast meal. Spoon it onto a plate, top with a generous serving of chili, vegetable stew, or sautéed vegetables, and you'll be eating in no time. You can serve cooked polenta warm, or let it cool for about 15 to 20 minutes until it becomes firm and then bake it. This step turns the polenta golden brown and makes it crispy on the outside and creamy on the inside.

Stovetop Polenta

In this recipe polenta is mixed with a small amount of water before adding it to the pot to keep it from becoming lumpy.

$1/2$ cup cornmeal
2 cups water
Pinch of salt
1 teaspoon olive oil

Combine the cornmeal and $1/2$ cup of the water in a bowl. In a 4-quart saucepan, bring the remaining $1^1/2$ cups of water to a boil. Add the salt. Stir in the wet cornmeal. Reduce the heat to the lowest setting and simmer for 10 to 15 minutes, stirring frequently, until the polenta is thick and creamy and loses its grittiness. If it becomes too stiff and dry during cooking, add a small amount of water, 1 tablespoon at a time, and keep stirring.

When ready, remove from the heat, stir in the olive oil, and serve.

Microwaved Polenta

Grains cooked in a microwave go wild, so make sure you use a large microwave-safe container (if you increase this recipe, you'll need an even larger bowl).

$\frac{1}{2}$ cup cornmeal
2 cups water
Pinch of salt
1 teaspoon olive oil

In a 1-quart (4-cup) microwavable bowl, whisk together the cornmeal, water, and salt. Cook on high for 5 minutes. Stir, and then microwave on high for an additional 2 minutes. Remove the polenta from the microwave and let it rest for 1 minute. The polenta should be the consistency of pudding. If it appears watery, microwave for an additional 1 to 2 minutes. Remove from the microwave, stir in the oil, and serve.

Baked Polenta Squares

PREPARATION TIME: 3 MINUTES
MAKES 1 TO 2 SERVINGS

Baked polenta is heavenly! Top it with slices of sautéed portobello mushrooms for a fine-tasting gourmet meal. Use baked polenta as a side dish for chili, or serve it for dessert drizzled with maple syrup.

2 servings of cooked, cooled polenta (see recipe for Stovetop
   Polenta, page 150, or Microwaved Polenta, page 151)
Olive oil

Preheat the oven to 375°F.

Spread the hot, cooked polenta onto a plate so that it's about 1/2 inch thick. When the polenta is cool, cut it into two 4-inch squares or triangles and place the pieces on a lightly oiled baking sheet.

Brush the polenta with oil, and bake for 20 to 25 minutes without turning until the top is slightly golden.

Quinoa

Quinoa (KEEN-wah) is a small, quick-cooking grain extremely high in protein, calcium, and phosphorus. Cultivated in South America for thousands of years, quinoa was a cornerstone of the Inca diet. It has a naturally occurring bitter coating that is mostly removed during processing, but the grain still needs a quick cold-water rinse to eliminate any bitter residue it might remain. As quinoa cooks, the external germ, which forms a band around each grain, spirals out, forming a tiny crescent-shaped "tail," similar to a bean sprout. Although the grain itself is soft and creamy, the tail is slightly crunchy, providing a unique texture to complement quinoa's delicate, nutty flavor.

Stovetop Quinoa

PREPARATION TIME: 10 MINUTES
COOKING TIME: 12 TO 15 MINUTES
MAKES ABOUT 2 CUPS

Quinoa cooks more quickly than rice and is just as easy to make. Add it to soups and stews, mound it on a plate and top with a stir-fry, or try mixing it with a bowl of cooked vegetables.

1 cup water or vegetable stock
1/4 teaspoon salt
1/2 cup quinoa, thoroughly rinsed and drained*

Bring water or stock and salt to a boil in a medium saucepan. Stir in the rinsed quinoa. Cover, reduce the heat to low, and simmer 12 to 15 minutes, until the liquid is absorbed and the quinoa is just tender. Before serving, fluff it with a fork.

*NOTE: To rinse quinoa, place the grain in a large bowl. Pour water on top to cover and swirl the seeds around vigorously with your hand. Drain through a fine-meshed strainer (you can purchase a strainer in most supermarket kitchen sections for a few dollars), and return the grains to the bowl. Repeat the process several times. Drain well.

Whole-Grain Couscous

PREPARATION TIME: 5 MINUTES
STEEPING TIME: 10 MINUTES
MAKES 1$^1/_2$ CUPS

This versatile, light grain is great hot or cold. Use it as a salad or a main dish with vegetables. It expands to about three times the original amount when you add water. Always set the couscous in a container and then pour the boiling water on top. Don't pour the couscous into the pot of boiling water or you may wind up with mush. Fluff with a fork before serving.

$^1/_2$ cup whole-grain couscous
Pinch of salt
$^1/_2$ cup boiling water

To a medium bowl, add the couscous and salt, then stir. Pour $^1/_2$ cup boiling water on top. Immediately cover tightly with a lid or a plate, and let the couscous sit for 10 minutes, or until all of the liquid is absorbed. Stir to fluff the grains. If the grains are still crunchy, add 1 to 2 tablespoons of boiling water, cover, and let the couscous steep for another 5 minutes. If it seems dry, add a tiny amount of oil to improve its texture.

Millet

PREPARATION TIME: 8 MINUTES
COOKING TIME: 25 TO 30 MINUTES
MAKES ABOUT 1 1/2 CUPS

Millet is used in Near Eastern and African cooking. It is a tiny, inexpensive grain that resembles couscous when cooked. Millet works well for patties and pilafs.

1/2 cup millet
1 1/2 cups water
Pinch of salt

In a medium pot, over medium heat, toast the millet, stirring constantly for 1 to 2 minutes, until the millet begins to brown and gives off a nutty aroma. Add the water and salt. Bring to a boil, reduce the heat, cover, and simmer for 25 to 30 minutes. If the millet is still a little crunchy, add 2 tablespoons boiling water and continue cooking for another 5 minutes. Fluff with a fork before serving.

Stovetop Cooking Guide for Grains

Whole grains are best stored in the refrigerator or freezer. Preparing more than will be needed for a specific meal gives you leftovers for a later meal. Cooked grains will keep refrigerated for 3 to 4 days.

Great Ideas for Grains

* Serve grains drizzled with a little olive oil.
* Sauté raw grain in oil with chopped onion until the onion is soft before adding the cooking liquid.
* Bring the water or stock to a boil and add a pinch of herbs and spices.

* Stir toasted sesame seeds, chopped nuts, or dried bits of fruit into cooked grains.

* Serve grains with sauces or gravies.

GRAIN (1 CUP)	WATER (CUPS)	COOKING TIME	YIELD (CUPS)
Barley	3	45–50 minutes	$3^1/_2$
Basmati rice (brown)	2	35–40 minutes	3
Brown rice	2	40–45 minutes	3
Buckwheat (kasha)	2	15 minutes	2
Cornmeal (polenta)	4–$4^1/_2$	10–15 minutes	4
Couscous (whole-grain)	1	10 minutes	2
Millet	3	25–30 minutes	$3^1/_2$
Quinoa*	2	15–20 minutes	$2^3/_4$

*Thoroughly rinse several times before cooking.

NINE

Pasta

Pasta is probably the first dish we think of for a quick and easy meal, and it seems that almost everyone loves it. Indeed, it's true that "friends who meet over noodles, meet in harmony" (Zao Noodle Bar). So cook up a pot of noodles, choose a sauce, and consider inviting your friends to dinner!

Pasta with Alfredo Sauce

PREPARATION TIME: 20 MINUTES
MAKES 2 TO 3 SERVINGS

Here is a rich new version of alfredo sauce, without the cream and cheese!

12 ounces soft silken tofu
1 or 2 garlic cloves, minced
1 tablespoon toasted sesame tahini
1 tablespoon mellow brown rice miso
$1/4$ teaspoon cayenne
$1/4$ to $1/2$ teaspoon freshly grated nutmeg
1 cup soy milk
Salt
6 to 9 ounces fettuccine
Fresh parsley, minced

To a medium saucepan, add the tofu, garlic, tahini, miso, cayenne, nutmeg, and soy milk. Whip with a wire whisk or fork until creamy. Gently heat over low or medium-low heat, stirring occasionally. Salt to taste.

Cook the fettuccine in a large pot of boiling water for 8 to 10 minutes, stirring occasionally, until al dente. Drain. Transfer the pasta to a large bowl. Stir in the sauce, and serve in shallow bowls, sprinkled with parsley.

Pasta with Marinara Sauce, Tempeh, and Black Olives

PREPARATION TIME: 25 MINUTES

MAKES 2 SERVINGS

Here tempeh cooks in a robust Mediterranean pasta sauce that tastes like it simmered on Grandma's stove for hours.

6 ounces multigrain tempeh
2 tablespoons olive oil
1 cup chopped onion
1 cup diced celery (about 3 ribs)
2 or 3 garlic cloves, thinly sliced
2$\frac{1}{2}$ cups water
One 6-ounce can tomato paste
1 tablespoon soy sauce
1$\frac{1}{2}$ teaspoons dried oregano
1 teaspoon dried thyme
$\frac{1}{2}$ to 1 teaspoon red pepper flakes
$\frac{1}{2}$ cup pitted, sliced black olives*
6 ounces spaghetti or rotelle
2 to 4 tablespoons chopped, fresh parsley

Cut tempeh into $\frac{1}{2}$-inch cubes. Warm 1 tablespoon of the oil in a medium skillet over medium heat. Add tempeh and brown on all sides, turning with a spatula several times. Cook for about 5 minutes. Place the tempeh in a small bowl, and set aside.

Warm the remaining 1 tablespoon of oil in the same skillet over medium heat. Add the onion and celery. Sauté for 3 to 5 minutes, until the onion is soft, stirring frequently. Add the garlic and sauté 30 seconds longer. Stir in the water, tomato paste, soy sauce, oregano, thyme, red pepper flakes, and olives.

Add the tempeh, and cook, uncovered, over medium heat at a

gentle boil for 15 minutes, stirring occasionally. Reduce the heat to a simmer, and cook for 3 more minutes. Remove from the heat.

While the sauce is simmering, cook the pasta in a large pot of boiling water for 8 to 10 minutes, stirring occasionally, until al dente. Drain. Divide the pasta between 2 shallow bowls. Spoon on the sauce, top with chopped parsley, and serve.

*NOTE: Oil-cured olives sold at olive bars or in jars are best, but canned, sliced olives work, too.

Chinese Vegetable Lo Mein with Tofu

PREPARATION TIME: 20 MINUTES

MAKES 2 SERVINGS

In this Asian-inspired pasta dish, cooked noodles are added to the skillet with vegetables during the final sauté. This step allows the noodles to gather flavors from the bottom of the pan.

- 6 ounces linguine
- 1 teaspoon toasted sesame oil
- 1 tablespoon olive oil
- 4 ounces extra-firm tofu, drained, patted dry, and cut into $1/2$-inch cubes
- 3 to 4 cups trimmed and thinly sliced regular or baby bok choy (use the stems)
- 1 small carrot, thinly sliced
- $1/4$ cup green peas
- 1 or 2 teaspoons minced fresh ginger
- 1 large garlic clove, minced
- $1^{1}/_2$ tablespoons soy sauce
- 2 scallions, chopped (use both the white and green parts)

Cook the linguine in a pot of boiling salted water for 8 to 10 minutes, stirring occasionally, until al dente. Drain. Transfer the noodles to a large bowl and add the sesame oil. Toss to coat the noodles with the oil. Set aside.

Warm 1 teaspoon of the olive oil in a medium skillet over medium heat. Add the tofu and stir-fry for about 5 minutes, until golden on all sides. Add the tofu to the noodles.

Reheat the skillet over medium-high heat with the remaining 2 teaspoons of olive oil. Add the bok choy and carrot. Stir-fry for 1 minute to soften the vegetables.

Add the peas, ginger, garlic, and 1 tablespoon of the soy sauce. Continue cooking 2 to 3 minutes, until the vegetables are tender.

Add the noodles to the skillet. Add the remaining $1/2$ tablespoon of soy sauce, and stir to combine the noodles with the vegetables. Sprinkle with the scallions, and serve at once.

Penne with White Beans and Greens

Penne is a good pasta choice, because it catches the olive oil and juice from the tomatoes. This meal is a top-notch combination of simple ingredients.

1 tablespoon olive oil
1 medium onion, diced (about 1 1/2 cups)
3 large garlic cloves, minced
5 cups chopped escarole or Swiss chard
Dash of salt and pinch of ground black pepper
One 15-ounce can whole tomatoes, with their juice
One 15-ounce can white beans or navy beans, drained
6 to 9 ounces penne
1 tablespoon fresh lemon juice

In a medium skillet, heat the oil. Add the onions and sauté 5 minutes over medium heat, until translucent. Add the garlic and cook 1 minute longer. Stir in the escarole, salt, and pepper. Cook for 3 to 5 minutes, covered, until the greens are bright green, wilted, and reduced by at least half. Add the liquid from the tomatoes, and coarsely chop the tomatoes with a knife right in the can. Stir the tomatoes and beans into the skillet, and bring the sauce to a gentle simmer.

Cook the penne in boiling water, stirring occasionally, for 8 to 10 minutes, until al dente. Drain. Stir the lemon juice into the sauce. Divide the pasta among 4 serving bowls. Top with the sauce, and serve at once.

Soba Noodles with Broccoli and Peanut Sauce

PREPARATION TIME: 15 MINUTES
MAKES 2 TO 3 SERVINGS

The broccoli in this recipe will be crunchy. If you prefer tender broccoli, add it to the pot a minute earlier. Serve the dish sprinkled with small pieces of seasoned baked tofu if you wish (but be sure to prepare the Peanut Sauce first).

4 to 6 ounces soba noodles
8 ounces broccoli florets, cut into bite-size pieces (about
   2$^{1}/_{2}$ cups)*
$^{1}/_{2}$ cup Peanut Sauce (recipe follows)
$^{1}/_{2}$ cup diced red bell pepper
$^{1}/_{4}$ cup chopped fresh cilantro or fresh parsley

Bring a pot of water to a rapid boil. Cook the pasta for 1 minute less than indicated on the package, and then add the broccoli to the boiling water. Continue cooking 1 minute longer until the noodles are al dente and the broccoli is bright green. Drain thoroughly in a colander and transfer the noodles and broccoli to a large bowl.

Add the Peanut Sauce and the red bell pepper. Stir to coat the noodles. Serve sprinkled with cilantro. Extra sauce will keep in the refrigerator for a week.

*NOTE: If you use frozen broccoli, defrost it first.

Peanut Sauce

This sauce is also delicious drizzled on a steaming sweet potato, cooked greens, or warm rice. Try it over crisp cabbage slaw.

$1/2$ cup natural-style peanut butter
1 tablespoon soy sauce
1 teaspoon seasoned rice vinegar*
$1/4$ teaspoon red pepper flakes
$1/4$ teaspoon finely minced garlic
$1/4$ teaspoon finely minced fresh ginger
About $1/3$ to $1/2$ cup hot water

In a small bowl, combine the peanut butter, soy sauce, rice vinegar, red pepper flakes, garlic, and ginger. Add enough hot water, a tablespoon at a time, to achieve a smooth sauce. Set aside.

*NOTE: Seasoned rice vinegar is sweetened with sugar. If you are using regular rice vinegar, add about $1/2$ teaspoon of sugar or natural sweetener to the peanut sauce.

One-Pot Pasta

PREPARATION TIME: 10 MINUTES
MAKES 1 SERVING

This meal shows you how to boil pasta and vegetables simultaneously in one pot for a quick meal.

    3 ounces fettuccine or udon noodles
    1 1/2 to 2 cups green beans, cut into thirds
    1 small carrot, thinly sliced (about 3/4 cup)
    1 tablespoon soy sauce
    1 tablespoon toasted sesame oil
    1/2 teaspoon toasted sesame seeds*
    Prepared baked tofu (page 37) (optional)
    Red pepper flakes

Bring a large pot of water to a boil. Add the fettuccine or udon, green beans, and carrots. Cook for 8 to 10 minutes, until the pasta is al dente. Drain (if any water remains in the pot, wipe the pot dry).

Return the vegetables and pasta to the pot and toss with the soy sauce, toasted sesame oil, and sesame seeds. Add pieces of prepared baked tofu, if using, and sprinkle with red pepper flakes to taste. Serve immediately.

*NOTE: In a small, dry skillet, toast the sesame seeds over moderate heat for 3 to 4 minutes, stirring or shaking the pan constantly, until the seeds are lightly browned. Immediately remove the seeds from the skillet to stop the cooking process.

TEN

Stovetop Meals—
Stews, Chili, and Sautés

We've probably all found ourselves standing in the spotlight of an open refrigerator searching for a meal that isn't there and settling for a tablespoon of peanut butter. In this chapter, you'll find new culinary solutions to your hunger. Many of the dishes are served over cooked grain.

Lickety-Split Burger Hash

PREPARATION TIME: 20 MINUTES
MAKES 2 SERVINGS

If you're looking for something more than a burger on a bun, this dish is a tasty choice. The recipe uses crumbled vegan burgers and cremini mushrooms, the dark brown button mushrooms available in most grocery stores. Serve over cooked noodles or another simple, cooked grain.

1 tablespoon olive oil
$1/4$ cup chopped onion
$3/4$ cup chopped red bell pepper
2 cups finely chopped cremini mushrooms (about 5 ounces)
2 vegan burger patties, thawed and chopped (about 5 ounces)
$1/2$ cup tomato sauce
1 teaspoon Dijon mustard
$1/2$ to 1 teaspoon pure maple syrup
Salt and ground black pepper

Warm the oil in a medium skillet over medium heat. Add the onion and bell pepper. Cover and cook for 5 minutes, or until the vegetables are soft.

Add the mushrooms and cook for 3 minutes, stirring occasionally. Stir in the vegan burgers, tomato sauce, mustard, and maple syrup. Add salt and pepper to taste. Simmer for 5 minutes, or until hot. Serve immediately.

Déjà Vu Sloppy Joes

PREPARATION TIME: 35 TO 40 MINUTES
MAKES 3 SERVINGS

Here is a fast version of a dish reminiscent of grade school cafeterias. The recipe highlights versatile tofu, and it's tasty enough to make you want seconds.

8 ounces firm tofu
$1/2$ cup chopped onion
1 or 2 garlic cloves, minced
1 tablespoon olive oil
$3/4$ cup chopped bell pepper
1 large tomato, diced (about 1 cup)
$1/2$ can tomato paste (3 ounces)
$1/4$ cup water
$1/2$ teaspoon ground cumin
$1/2$ teaspoon dried oregano
$1/2$ teaspoon chili powder
$1/2$ teaspoon brown sugar or natural sweetener
$1/4$ teaspoon red pepper flakes
$1/2$ teaspoon salt
Ground black pepper
3 whole-grain hamburger rolls, sliced in half and lightly toasted
Chopped fresh parsley

Sandwich the tofu between two plates and rest a heavy book or weight on the top plate. Press for 15 minutes, then drain the expressed liquid from the bottom plate.

In a medium bowl, crumble the pressed tofu, and set aside.

In a medium skillet, heat the oil on medium heat. Add the onion and garlic. Sauté for 3 to 5 minutes, until the onion is translucent. Add the bell pepper and continue to cook for 5 more minutes, stirring occasionally.

Add the tofu, diced tomatoes, tomato paste, water, cumin, oregano, chili powder, brown sugar, red pepper flakes, and salt. Simmer for 10 minutes. Add black pepper to taste.

Spoon the mixture onto the toasted rolls for open-faced Sloppy Joes. Sprinkle with chopped parsley.

Edamame Stir-Fry with Rice and Mustard Sauce

Even though the sauce for this stir-fry is made from a few everyday staples, it gives the dish surprising zing. You can use noodles in place of the rice if you like. Prepare the Mustard Sauce before you start the stir-fry. A slice of melon or sliced pear makes a good dessert.

$1/2$ cup frozen, shelled edamame
1 teaspoon olive oil
1 red or yellow bell pepper, cut into thin strips (about 1 cup)
2 small carrots, thinly sliced ($1/2$ cup)
2 cups cooked rice
Mustard Sauce (recipe follows)

Cook the edamame according to package directions, and set aside. Heat the olive oil in a medium skillet over medium heat. Add the bell pepper and carrots, and stir-fry for 3 to 5 minutes. Add the edamame and heat 1 minute longer. Stir in the rice and add 2 tablespoons of Mustard Sauce. Heat thoroughly for 2 minutes, stirring occasionally, until hot. Spoon the stir-fry into bowls and drizzle with additional Mustard Sauce.

Mustard Sauce

2 tablespoons soy sauce
2 tablespoons Dijon mustard
1¹/₂ tablespoons water
1¹/₂ tablespoons toasted sesame oil
1 tablespoon pure maple syrup

Combine the ingredients in a small bowl, and set aside.

Indonesian Tempeh Stew

Once you prepare this fragrant stew, you'll see how quickly and easily it goes together. The coconut milk makes a rich, creamy sauce. Serve the stew over freshly cooked rice or Japanese udon noodles.

6 to 8 ounces multigrain tempeh
2 tablespoons olive oil
$1/2$ cup finely chopped onion
2 garlic cloves, minced (about 2 teaspoons)
$1/2$ teaspoon fresh minced ginger
$1/4$ teaspoon red pepper flakes
2 cups peeled and diced sweet potato ($1/2$-inch pieces)
$1/4$ cup snow peas, strings removed and sliced ($1/2$-inch pieces)*
$1/2$ cup water
1 cup canned crushed tomatoes
$1 1/2$ teaspoons soy sauce
$3/4$ cup unsweetened light coconut milk
Salt and ground black pepper
1 tablespoon chopped fresh cilantro or fresh parsley
1 tablespoon freshly squeezed lime juice

Cut the tempeh into $1/2$-inch cubes. Warm 1 tablespoon oil in a medium skillet over medium-high heat. Add the tempeh and brown on all sides for about 5 minutes, turning occasionally with a spatula. Transfer the tempeh to a plate and set aside.

Reduce the heat to medium and add the remaining 1 table-spoon oil to the skillet. Add the onion and sauté for 3 minutes, or until the onion is translucent. Add the garlic, ginger, and pepper flakes, and sauté for 2 minutes longer. Stir in the sweet potato, snow peas, water, tomatoes, soy sauce, and the browned tempeh.

Cover and cook on medium heat for 12 to 15 minutes, stirring occasionally, until the vegetables are tender.

Uncover, and reduce the heat to low. Add the coconut milk and salt and pepper to taste. Simmer, stirring occasionally, until thickened, about 4 to 5 minutes. Remove from the heat and stir in the cilantro and lime juice. Serve hot.

*NOTE: If you can't find fresh snow peas, substitute green peas and add them to the stew when you add the coconut milk. They only need warming and will remain bright green if not overcooked.

Coconut fat will naturally separate from coconut milk in the can. Shake the can well before using. Unused coconut milk can be refrigerated in a covered container for three days, or it can be frozen and will keep for six months.

Quinoa Corn and Potato Stew

PREPARATION TIME: 25 MINUTES
MAKES 2 SERVINGS

Protein-rich quinoa combined with the flavor of sweet corn and potatoes makes a speedy main-dish meal. Serve it with a crisp green leaf salad.

1 tablespoon olive oil
1/3 cup chopped onion
1/2 cup chopped red or green bell pepper
1/2 cup quinoa, thoroughly rinsed and drained (see page 153)
1 cup water
1/4 teaspoon salt
1/2 teaspoon ground cumin
1 small red or yellow potato cut into 1/2-inch dice or smaller (about 3/4 cup)
1/2 cup corn kernels
2 tablespoons chopped fresh cilantro or fresh parsley
Red pepper flakes

Warm the oil in a medium saucepan over medium heat. Add the onion and bell pepper and sauté for 3 to 5 minutes, until the onion is translucent, stirring frequently. Add the drained quinoa and cook, stirring constantly, for 3 minutes.

Add the water, salt, cumin, and potato. Bring the pot to a boil; reduce to a simmer, cover, and cook for 10 minutes. Add the corn, cover, and continue cooking for 3 to 5 minutes, until the liquid is absorbed and the grain is tender.

If all the liquid is absorbed and the quinoa is not yet tender, stir in 2 or 3 tablespoons of boiling water, cover, and continue simmering until done. Be careful not to overcook the quinoa or it will become glutinous.

Serve sprinkled with chopped cilantro and a shake of red pepper flakes.

Ratatouille

This recipe makes a rich, chunky vegetable stew. Serve the dish in shallow bowls over creamy polenta or mashed potatoes, or, if you prefer, serve it with French bread to dip in the savory juices. It's even better eaten at room temperature the next day. It will keep, covered, in the refrigerator for 2 to 3 days.

$^1/_2$ small eggplant, sliced in half lengthwise, unpeeled
1$^1/_4$ tablespoons olive oil
$^1/_2$ small yellow onion, thinly sliced and separated into rings
3 or 4 garlic cloves, minced
$^1/_2$ small red or yellow bell pepper, sliced into $^1/_4$-inch strips
1 medium zucchini, cut into $^1/_4$-inch-thick slices
One 14-ounce can whole tomatoes, with their juice
$^3/_4$ cup garbanzo beans, drained and rinsed
$^1/_2$ teaspoon dried thyme leaves
Salt and ground black pepper
Chopped fresh parsley

Preheat the oven to 350°F. Lightly oil a large baking sheet.

Score the flesh of the eggplant half, brush the inside surface with $^1/_4$ tablespoon olive oil, and place it, cut side down, on the baking sheet. Bake for 20 to 30 minutes, or until the eggplant is soft and the skin has shriveled.

While the eggplant bakes, prepare the remaining vegetables. Warm the remaining 1 tablespoon of oil in a large skillet over medium heat. Add the onion and sauté for 3 to 5 minutes, stirring occasionally, until translucent. Stir in the garlic and sauté for 1 minute. Add the bell pepper and zucchini. Continue cooking for 5 to 8 minutes, stirring frequently, until the vegetables begin to soften.

(continued)

When the eggplant is ready, remove it from the oven, let it cool slightly, and cut into bite-size pieces.

Chop the tomatoes in the can, and add them to the skillet. Stir in the eggplant, garbanzo beans, and thyme. Add salt and pepper to taste. Cover, and cook for 15 minutes, until the vegetables are tender and the flavors have mingled. Sprinkle with parsley and serve hot or at room temperature.

A Creamy Eggplant Sandwich

Use the remaining eggplant half to make an eggplant sandwich. Cut the eggplant into $1/4$-inch-thick slices, brush with olive oil, place on a lightly oiled baking sheet, and bake at 400°F. for 15 minutes, or until the eggplant is fork-tender. Spread one slice of bread with mustard and vegan mayonnaise. Add the eggplant slices, lettuce, and tomato. Top with the second slice of bread. Cooked eggplant will keep, covered and refrigerated, for 2 to 3 days.

Seitan Sauté
with Pineapple

Here is a meal that delivers a lot of flavor with little effort. Serve over a mound of freshly cooked rice.

2 teaspoons olive oil
1/2 medium onion, chopped (about 1/2 cup)
2 garlic cloves, minced
1 teaspoon garam masala*
1/2 cup chopped red bell pepper
2 1/2 cups broccoli florets, cut into bite-size pieces
4 ounces seitan, preferably a seasoned variety, finely chopped
    (1 cup)
One 10-ounce can crushed pineapple, unsweetened
1 tablespoon natural-style peanut butter
1/4 cup light coconut milk
Salt and ground black pepper
Unsalted, dry roasted peanuts
Chopped fresh cilantro

Warm the oil in a large skillet on medium heat. Add the onion and sauté for 3 to 5 minute, or until translucent. Add the garlic and garam marsala and sauté another minute, stirring constantly.

Stir in the bell pepper, broccoli, and seitan, and cook for 1 to 2 minutes. Add the pineapple, peanut butter, and coconut milk. Simmer over medium heat for 8 to 10 minutes, or until the vegetables are tender-crisp and the sauce begins to thicken slightly. Add the salt and pepper to taste. Serve topped with the crushed peanuts and cilantro.

(continued)

*NOTE: Garam masala is a spice blend used in Indian cooking that usually includes cardamom, cinnamon, cloves, coriander, cumin, and black pepper. It's expensive, so look for it in the bulk section of a natural food supermarket, where it costs much less and can be purchased in tiny amounts.

Barbecued Beans

Serve Barbecued Beans with a slice of warm molasses bread or try spooning the beans over corn bread. Turn the meal into a picnic by adding a side of coleslaw.

One 15-ounce can pinto beans, drained and rinsed
2 vegan hot dogs, sliced into $1/4$-inch rounds
$3/4$ cup Barbecue Sauce (recipe follows)

To a medium-size saucepan, add the pinto beans, vegan hot dogs, and Barbecue Sauce. Simmer for 10 minutes.

Barbecue Sauce

$1/4$ cup finely chopped onion
1 garlic clove, minced
2 tablespoons soy sauce
2 tablespoons cider vinegar
2 tablespoons ketchup
2 tablespoons orange juice
1 tablespoon Dijon mustard
1 tablespoon unsulfured blackstrap molasses
$1/4$ teaspoon dried thyme
$1/4$ teaspoon ground black pepper

Combine all the ingredients in a small saucepan. Simmer, uncovered, for 10 minutes, stirring often. It will keep refrigerated for two weeks.

Italian White Bean and Vegetable Stew

Fennel gives this stew a distinctive, delicate flavor. For something extra, add ¾ cup chopped soy sausage. Serve with a garden salad and raspberry sorbet for dessert.

1 tablespoon olive oil
1 medium yellow onion, chopped (about 1½ cups)
4 garlic cloves, minced
2 teaspoons fennel seeds
½ teaspoon salt
One 28-ounce can whole tomatoes, with their juice
1 large potato, peeled and cut into ½-inch dice (about 3 cups)
½ teaspoon dried rosemary leaves
2 medium carrots, thinly sliced (about 1½ cups)
One 15-ounce can Great Northern, cannellini, or navy beans, rinsed and drained
3 tablespoons minced fresh parsley

Warm the olive oil in a large saucepan over medium heat. Add the onion, garlic, fennel seeds, and salt. Cover and cook for 10 minutes on medium-low heat, stirring occasionally.

Chop the tomatoes in the can. Add the tomatoes, potatoes, and rosemary to the saucepan. Cover the pot and simmer for 10 minutes, stirring occasionally. Add the carrots and continue gently simmering, covered, for 10 minutes, or until the vegetables are tender. Add the beans and parsley. Continue cooking and stir for 1 or 2 minutes, until hot. Serve immediately.

Lentil Stew with Butternut Squash

PREPARATION TIME: 15 MINUTES
COOKING TIME: 35 TO 45 MINUTES
MAKES 2 SERVINGS

The orange juice, orange zest, and a pinch of cinnamon add sparkle to earthy lentils. Spoon the stew over cooked basmati rice or spiral noodles and serve with a side of cooked greens for a top-notch meal.

   $1/2$ small butternut squash (about 2 cups chopped)
   1 tablespoon olive oil
   $1/2$ onion, chopped
   1 garlic clove, chopped
   $1/8$ to $1/4$ teaspoon cayenne
   $1/2$ teaspoon ground cumin
   $1^1/2$ cups water
   $1/2$ cup brown lentils
   $1/2$ teaspoon salt
   $1/4$ teaspoon ground cinnamon
   1 teaspoon orange zest, minced*
   $1/4$ cup orange juice

   Place the squash cut side down on the countertop and slice off the outer peel. Scoop out the seeds and discard. Coarsely chop the squash and set aside.
   Heat the oil over medium heat in a medium pot. Add the onion and garlic and sauté for 3 minutes, stirring occasionally. Add the cayenne and cumin, and continue cooking for 2 minutes.
   Add the water, lentils, salt, and squash. Bring to a boil, reduce the heat, cover, and simmer for 35 to 45 minutes, or until the lentils are tender. Add the cinnamon and orange zest. Cook 2 min-

(continued)

utes longer. Remove the pot from the heat, and add the orange juice and stir. Serve immediately. This dish will keep in the refrigerator, covered, for 2 to 3 days.

*NOTE: Zest is the thin bright outer skin of citrus fruit, without the white undercoat. Use a vegetable peeler or sharp knife to shave off the zest, taking care not to peel off the bitter whitish tissue under the rind. If you are uncertain of the source of the fruit (whether it's organic or not), use hot water to remove whatever may have been sprayed on the surface.

Red-Bean Chili with Corn

PREPARATION TIME: 15 MINUTES
MAKES 3 SERVINGS

Serve this colorful chili with a handful of tortilla chips on the side, and finish the meal with a sliced mango or a tropical fruit smoothie.

$1/4$ cup hot water
$1/4$ cup whole-grain bulghur wheat
$1^1/2$ tablespoons olive oil
1 small yellow onion, chopped ($1^1/2$ cups)
2 garlic cloves, chopped
1 teaspoon ground cumin
$1^1/2$ teaspoons chili powder
$1/8$ teaspoon cayenne
$1/4$ cup chopped bell pepper (red, yellow, or green)
One 15-ounce can whole tomatoes, with their juice
1 cup corn kernels
One 4-ounce can mild diced green chilies
One 14-ounce can kidney beans, drained and rinsed ($1^1/2$ cups)
Salt and ground black pepper
Chopped fresh cilantro

In a small saucepan, bring the water to boil. Remove from the heat, add the bulghur, cover, and set aside for 10 minutes, until the liquid is absorbed and the grain is tender.

Warm the olive oil in a medium skillet on medium heat. Sauté the onion, garlic, cumin, chili powder, and cayenne, stirring frequently, for 3 minutes. When the onion is translucent, stir in the bell pepper and continue cooking 3 minutes longer, stirring occasionally. Chop the tomatoes right in the can and add them to the mixture. Stir in the corn, green chilies, and beans, and heat thoroughly on low. When the bulghur is ready, add it to the pan. Cover and simmer for 2 to 3 minutes. Add salt and pepper to taste. Serve sprinkled with cilantro.

ELEVEN

Pizza and Oven Meals

Get out your pot holders and turn on the oven! Here are recipes for celebrated one-dish meals that give you something extra—plenty of leftovers.

Pizza Dough

PREPARATION TIME: 25 MINUTES
RISING TIME: 30 TO 40 MINUTES
BAKING TIME: 8 TO 10 MINUTES
MAKES ONE 12-INCH PIZZA (1 TO 4 SERVINGS)

Anyone can make a fresh, wholesome pizza from scratch—dough and all—for a fraction of the cost of commercial pizza. Today, pizza is experiencing a cultural and nutritional overhaul, and vegans can delight in lively, light-tasting pizza without a lava flow of cheese.

This basic dough is made with half unbleached white flour and half whole-wheat flour. The kind of flour you use for the dough will determine the texture. You can use all-purpose white flour or even pastry flour if you like.

For something extra, add a tablespoon of toasted sesame seeds to the mixture when you add the flour. For more crunch, sprinkle a tablespoon of cornmeal on the baking pan before you transfer the dough to the pan.

$^1/_2$ cup warm water (110°F.)
$^1/_2$ teaspoon pure maple syrup
1 tablespoon active dry baking yeast (1 package)
2 tablespoons olive oil
$^1/_4$ teaspoon salt
$^1/_8$ teaspoon ground black pepper
$^1/_2$ cup whole-wheat flour
$^1/_2$ to $^3/_4$ cup unbleached white flour
1 to 4 tablespoons unbleached white flour for rolling out the dough

Yeast is fussy about temperature. If the water is too hot, the yeast will not cooperate. The water should be just about body temperature, barely warm to your hand. In a large bowl, combine the warm water and maple syrup. Stir in the yeast. Set it aside to proof (bubble and foam) for 10 to 12 minutes.

(continued)

Add the olive oil, salt, pepper, and whole-wheat flour. Mix well, gradually adding 1/2 cup of white flour. Use the other quarter cup if needed, adding the flour gradually to make a soft, workable dough that can be handled and does not stick to your hands.

Turn the dough out onto a lightly floured work surface and knead for 5 to 10 minutes, sprinkling in flour as needed to keep the dough from sticking to the surface. It is important to use as little flour as you can for the kneading, because too much flour makes the crust tough. When the dough is smooth, springy, and pliant, transfer it to an oiled bowl. Turn it once so the entire surface is coated. Cover with a towel, and set aside in a warm place to rise for 30 to 40 minutes, until it doubles in bulk.

While the dough is rising, prepare the topping.

When the dough is ready to use, preheat the oven to 450°F.

To shape the pizza into a 12-inch circle or rectangle, first form the dough into a ball. Place the ball on a lightly floured surface. With your hands or a rolling pin, press down and out from the center of the dough until the crust has reached the desired thickness. Transfer the dough to a lightly oiled baking pan. Add your chosen topping, and bake.

Thick or Thin Crust

If you like a thinner crust, roll out the dough, add the topping, and bake immediately. If you like a thicker crust, roll out the dough, place it on the baking pan, and let it rise for 8 to 10 minutes longer. Then add the topping and bake.

Tomato-and-Black-Olive Pizza

PREPARATION TIME: 15 MINUTES
MAKES ONE 12-INCH PIZZA (1 TO 4 SERVINGS)

Here is a classic rustic pizza topping. Spread the sauce on sparingly so that the dough shows through; otherwise the crust will be soggy on top. Pizza goes great with soup and salad, and, of course, leftover pizza makes a fast hand-to-mouth breakfast.

One 14-ounce can peeled, diced tomatoes, with their liquid
1 tablespoon balsamic vinegar
$^1/_2$ teaspoon ground black pepper
1 recipe Pizza Dough, ready to roll out (page 187)
$^1/_4$ cup sliced black olives
1 tablespoon chopped fresh basil

Preheat the oven to 450°F.

Empty the tomatoes into a sieve or colander set over a deep bowl. Stir the tomatoes several times to speed the draining, and reserve the tomato liquid.

Transfer the tomato liquid to a small saucepan and set the tomatoes aside. Add the vinegar and pepper to the saucepan and bring the mixture to a boil over high heat. Continue boiling, uncovered, for 4 to 5 minutes, until there is slightly more than $^1/_4$ cup of sauce. This step concentrates the flavors. Remove the pan from the heat and cool.

Roll out the dough and place it on a lightly oiled baking sheet. Scrape the sauce onto the dough, and spread it thinly over the top of the pizza. Scatter the tomatoes and olives over the sauce, and bake for 8 to 10 minutes, or until the crust is golden.

Remove the pizza from the oven; sprinkle with chopped fresh basil or chop together $^1/_4$ cup fresh flat-leaf parsley and $^1/_4$ teaspoon dried oregano and scatter it on top.

Pizza Toppings at Your Fingertips

You'll find grocery shelves overflowing with jars of condiments that make instant pizza toppings. Vegan pesto, vegan olive tapenade, salsas, oil-packed sun-dried tomatoes, capers, oil-packed artichoke hearts, and roasted red peppers make tasty additions to any pizza.

Caramelized Onion, Walnut, and Sage Pizza

The taste of sweet, slowly cooked onions is offset with crunchy walnuts and the earthy flavor of sage for a perfect pizza topping. The first time you make this recipe, keep an eye on the onions while they cook to see how the stove and the particular pan you use work together. Stir the onions occasionally until they begin to color, and then stir them frequently. If the onions begin to cook too quickly, lower the heat. If sticking becomes a problem, sprinkle in a little water.

1 tablespoon olive oil, plus more for brushing top of pizza dough*
2 large yellow onions, thinly sliced
$1/2$ teaspoon salt
Ground black pepper
1 garlic clove, finely chopped
1 or 2 tablespoons water
1 recipe Pizza Dough, ready to roll out (page 187)
$1/3$ cup walnuts, coarsely chopped
1 teaspoon dried sage leaves

Warm 1 tablespoon of olive oil in a medium skillet. Add the onion slices, salt, and a few pinches of pepper. Sauté over medium to medium-low heat, gently scraping the pan occasionally with a large spoon to keep the onions from sticking as they caramelize. After about 35 minutes, the onions should be golden and very sweet. Add the garlic and sauté for 5 minutes longer. Add 1 or 2 tablespoons of water to help scrape up the flavors left on the bottom of the pan. Set the onions aside to cool.

Preheat the oven to 450°F.

(continued)

Roll out the dough and place it on a lightly oiled baking pan; brush the top with olive oil. Spread the caramelized onions on the dough, and sprinkle on the walnuts. Bake the pizza for 8 to 10 minutes, until the crust is golden. Remove the pizza from the oven, and crumble the sage leaves over the top.

*NOTE: Whenever you make pizza without a sauce, brush some olive oil over the dough before adding the topping.

Pita bread also makes a very good base for quick, thin, and crispy pizzas.

Lasagna with Herbed Tofu

Lasagna is architectural cuisine at its best, a culinary construction built up in layers that's pleasing to the eye and the palate. This recipe may surprise you—the noodles are not boiled before assembling the dish, but cook in the oven as the lasagna bakes. Lasagna is a great make-ahead meal for sharing with friends. They'll have a hard time believing that the herbed tofu is not ricotta cheese.

Olive oil
1 medium eggplant, unpeeled and cut into $1/2$-inch rounds
Olive oil for brushing
$3^1/2$ to 4 cups Marinara Sauce (page 120) or store-bought sauce
16 ounces firm tofu, rinsed
1 teaspoon dried basil
1 teaspoon dried thyme
1 teaspoon dried oregano
1 teaspoon salt
$1/2$ teaspoon ground black pepper
10 ounces chopped frozen spinach
12 ounces lasagna noodles (about 12 noodles)

Preheat the oven to 400°F.

Lightly oil a baking sheet, lay the eggplant rounds in the sheet, brush them with olive oil, and bake uncovered for about 15 minutes, or until the eggplant is tender. Remove from the oven and reduce the heat to 350°F. In a few minutes, when the eggplant is cool enough to handle, cut the rounds into bite-size pieces. In a medium bowl, combine the eggplant and the marinara sauce. Set aside.

(continued)

In a second bowl, crumble the tofu and mash it with a fork. Add the basil, thyme, oregano, salt, and pepper. Stir to combine. Boil ¼ inch of water in a medium pot. Add the spinach. Cover, reduce the heat, and simmer gently for 4 to 5 minutes, until tender. Drain well, pressing out any excess water. Add the spinach to the seasoned tofu.

Lightly oil a 9 × 13-inch ovenproof baking dish. Spread one fourth of the marinara sauce mixture on the bottom of the prepared baking dish. Cover with a layer of dry noodles, then add half of the tofu-spinach filling. Ladle on another fourth of the marinara sauce mixture. Repeat the layer of noodles, the rest of the tofu-spinach filling, and one fourth of the sauce. Finish with a final layer of noodles and the remaining sauce.

Cover tightly with foil and bake for 50 minutes (try to "tent" the foil so that it does not touch the tomato sauce). Uncover, and bake 10 minutes longer, or until the pasta is tender. Remove from the oven and let the lasagna set for 5 to 10 minutes before cutting.

Macaroni and "Cheese"

PREPARATION TIME: 15 TO 20 MINUTES
COOKING TIME: 25 TO 30 MINUTES
MAKES 4 SERVINGS

If you have fond memories of macaroni and cheese from your childhood, this protein-rich dish will more than satisfy your nostalgic longing. If you're new to vegan cooking you may wonder why the recipe does not use vegan cheese. Most vegan cheese does not melt well, so soft silken tofu is used instead to make a creamy sauce. Turmeric gives the macaroni a light golden color. If you don't have it in your cupboard, the dish will still taste fine without it.

8 ounces whole-wheat elbow macaroni
1 tablespoon olive oil
$^{1}/_{2}$ cup chopped yellow onion
2 large garlic cloves, minced
12 ounces soft silken tofu
1$^{1}/_{2}$ cups soy milk
1 tablespoon fresh lemon juice
1 tablespoon mellow light miso
$^{1}/_{2}$ teaspoon Dijon mustard
$^{1}/_{4}$ to $^{1}/_{2}$ teaspoon turmeric
$^{1}/_{4}$ teaspoon freshly grated nutmeg
$^{1}/_{4}$ teaspoon cayenne
Salt
Paprika
$^{1}/_{3}$ cup toasted almonds, chopped*

Preheat the oven to 375°F.

Cook the macaroni in a pot of salted boiling water for 8 to 10 minutes, until al dente. Drain and *do not rinse*. Set aside in a large bowl.

(continued)

Warm the olive oil in a medium saucepan over medium heat. Add the onion and sauté for 3 to 5 minutes, until translucent. Add the garlic, cook 1 minute longer, then remove from the heat. Add the tofu, soy milk, lemon juice, miso, mustard, turmeric, nutmeg, and cayenne. Whip with a wire whisk or process in a blender until creamy. Salt to taste. Pour the mixture over the macaroni. Stir well.

Transfer the macaroni mixture to a lightly oiled $1^1/_2$-quart baking dish. Cover with foil and bake for 25 to 30 minutes, or until hot. Remove from the oven. Garnish with a light dusting of paprika and sprinkle on the nuts. Let the dish sit for 5 minutes before serving.

*NOTE: Toast the nuts on a dry baking sheet in a preheated 350°F. oven for 5 minutes, or until fragrant and lightly browned. Remove them immediately from the pan to stop the cooking process.

Shepherd's Pie

PREPARATION TIME: 25 MINUTES
BAKING TIME: 20 TO 25 MINUTES
MAKES 2 TO 4 SERVINGS

This classic comfort food is especially welcome on a chilly winter night. The recipe highlights the sweet taste of parsnips with savory potatoes. You can vary the filling ingredients depending on your preferences and what you have on hand, and you can substitute tempeh or chopped veggie burgers for the seitan.

Mashed Potatoes

3 cups water
3 cups peeled, cubed russet potatoes*
4 large garlic cloves, peeled
1/2 teaspoon salt
1/2 cup soy milk

Filling

1 tablespoon, plus 2 teaspoons olive oil
1 medium onion, chopped
2 garlic cloves, minced
2 carrots, thinly sliced (1/4 inch thick or less), about 1 cup
2 parsnips, peeled and thinly sliced (1/4 inch thick or less), about 1 1/2 cups
1 teaspoon dried thyme leaves
6 ounces seitan, preferably a seasoned variety, finely chopped
1 cup potato stock
2 tablespoons soy sauce
1 tablespoon cornstarch, dissolved in 2 tablespoons potato stock
1/2 cup fresh or frozen green peas
Salt and ground black pepper
Paprika

(continued)

Prepare the mashed potatoes: In a saucepan, combine the water, potatoes, garlic, and salt, cover, and bring to a boil. Reduce the heat and simmer for 15 minutes, or until the potatoes are tender. Drain the potatoes, reserving the potato stock, which you will need for making the filling. Mash the potatoes in a large bowl with the soy milk. Set aside.

Preheat the oven to 375°F.

Heat 1 tablespoon oil in a large skillet over medium heat. Add the onion and sauté for 5 minutes, stirring frequently. Add the garlic, carrots, parsnips, and thyme, and sauté for 3 to 5 minutes, stirring occasionally. Add the seitan. Pour the potato stock into the skillet. Add the soy sauce. Stir in the cornstarch mixture, and simmer, stirring constantly, for 1 to 2 minutes, until the liquid thickens. Cover and cook on medium to medium-low heat for 5 to 10 minutes, until the carrots and parsnips are tender, stirring occasionally. Add the peas. Salt and pepper to taste. Transfer the filling to a lightly oiled 1 1/2-quart baking dish.

Spread the mashed potatoes over the top of the vegetables. Drizzle the remaining 2 teaspoons olive oil onto the potatoes and lightly sprinkle with paprika. Bake for 20 minutes, until the potatoes are hot and the top is lightly golden.

*NOTE: If you don't mind tiny brown flecks in your mashed potatoes, don't bother peeling them.

Stuffed Winter Squash

PREPARATION TIME: 30 MINUTES

BAKING TIME: 35 TO 40 MINUTES

MAKES 2 SERVINGS

Acorn squash stuffed with cooked rice and mushroom sauce is a delightful meal. Choose an acorn squash on the smaller side, as it will cook more quickly and may be more tender on the inside than a large one. Serve this dish with a side of steamed broccoli and ginger cookies for dessert.

Squash
- 1 medium acorn squash, cut in half and seeded
- 1 teaspoon olive oil
- 2 teaspoons pure maple syrup
- $1/2$ teaspoon ground cinnamon

Filling
- 1 tablespoon olive oil
- 1 cup finely chopped yellow onion
- 2 large garlic cloves, minced
- $1 1/2$ cups thinly sliced and chopped white mushrooms
- 1 tablespoon dried sage leaves
- $1/4$ teaspoon thyme
- 2 cups water or vegetable broth
- 2 tablespoons soy sauce
- 1 tablespoon cornstarch, dissolved in 2 tablespoons of water
- $1 1/2$ cups cooked rice
- Salt and ground black pepper
- $1/4$ cup chopped fresh parsley

Preheat the oven to 350°F.

Brush the inside of the squash halves with the oil and maple syrup. Sprinkle with the cinnamon. Place the squash cut side down

(continued)

in a baking dish and bake for 35 minutes, or until tender. While the squash bakes, prepare the filling.

Warm the olive oil in a medium skillet over medium heat. Add the onion and sauté for 8 to 10 minutes, or until soft, stirring occasionally. Add the garlic and cook 1 minute longer. Add the mushrooms, sage, and thyme. Continue sautéing for 2 to 3 minutes, until the mushrooms are tender and release their juices. Add the water or vegetable broth, and soy sauce. Simmer for 1 minute, to blend the flavors. Stir the cornstarch mixture, and add it to the skillet. Reduce the heat to medium-low and cook for 2 to 3 minutes, until the sauce thickens. Stir in the rice. Salt and pepper to taste.

Place each squash half in a shallow serving bowl. Spoon the rice mixture into the baked squash, top with chopped parsley, and serve immediately.

Crusty Tempeh Cutlets

PREPARATION TIME: 10 MINUTES
BAKING TIME: 60 MINUTES
MAKES 2 TO 3 SERVINGS

This is a not-to-miss dish! The tempeh is baked for an hour and then quickly sautéed. Bake the tempeh a day ahead, and you can have dinner ready in minutes the next evening. For a showstopper meal, add a baked sweet potato, applesauce, and sautéed greens. The cutlets make good leftovers eaten cold.

6 to 8 ounces multigrain tempeh, cut into thirds*
$^1/_3$ cup soy sauce
$^1/_3$ cup water
$1^1/_2$ tablespoons pure maple syrup
$^1/_3$ cup orange juice
1 clove garlic, minced
$^1/_2$ cup cornmeal
1 teaspoon dried thyme
1 teaspoon ground cumin
$^1/_8$ to $^1/_4$ teaspoon red pepper flakes
$^1/_8$ teaspoon salt
Dijon mustard
1 tablespoon olive oil

Preheat oven to 350°F.

Place the tempeh in the smallest baking pan you have that will hold it in a single layer. In a small bowl, combine the soy sauce, water, maple syrup, orange juice, and garlic. Pour the mixture over the tempeh. Cover tightly with foil and bake for 30 minutes. Remove from oven, turn the tempeh, replace the foil cover, and continue baking for 30 minutes longer. Transfer the tempeh to a plate to cool.

Pour the cornmeal onto a plate. Add the thyme, cumin, red pepper flakes, and salt. Stir to combine.

(continued)

Lightly brush both sides of the tempeh with mustard and coat with the seasoned cornmeal.

Warm the oil in a medium skillet on medium-high heat. Sizzle the tempeh until golden, about 1 minute for each side. Remove from the heat and serve immediately.

TWELVE

Desserts and Drinks

Your nonvegan friends may disagree with you over burgers and barbecues, but most of them will happily grab a fork and dig into dessert. If you're feeling s-t-r-e-s-s-e-d, turn the word around, and you'll see it spells *desserts*. Whip up these recipes to relax.

Oatmeal Walnut Gems

PREPARATION TIME: 15 MINUTES

BAKING TIME: 12 TO 15 MINUTES

MAKES ABOUT 1 1/2 DOZEN LARGE (2-INCH) COOKIES

The pleasure of eating warm cookies straight from the oven cannot be overstated. These cookies make it easy to pass by the long aisle in the supermarket full of commercial cookies with dubious ingredients. This recipe uses Ener-G Egg Replacer, a product sold in most natural food markets. You can also use any of the mixtures from the list of egg substitutes on page 205.

1 1/4 cups unbleached all-purpose flour
1 1/2 cups old-fashioned rolled oats
1 teaspoon baking powder
1/4 teaspoon ground cinnamon
1/4 teaspoon ground nutmeg
1/8 teaspoon salt
1/2 cup raisins
1/2 cup chopped walnuts
1/2 cup canola oil
3/4 cup firmly packed brown sugar or natural sweetener
1/4 cup soy milk or dairy-free milk
1 teaspoon pure vanilla extract
Ener-G Egg Replacer for 2 eggs

Preheat the oven to 350°F. Lightly oil a baking sheet.

In a large bowl, combine the flour, oats, baking powder, cinnamon, nutmeg, and salt. Stir well to combine. Add the raisins and nuts, and stir again.

To a medium bowl, add the oil, brown sugar, 1/4 cup soy milk, vanilla, and egg substitute. Stir to combine. Add the wet ingredients to the dry ingredients and blend well.

Drop the dough by spoonfuls onto the prepared baking sheet about 1 inch apart. Bake for 12 to 15 minutes, or until lightly browned.

Crack the Problem of Egg-Free Baking by Using Egg Substitutes

Eggs give baked goods a light texture and hold the ingredients together. Any of the following mixtures can replace 1 egg in baking. It may take some experimenting to find out which works best in a particular recipe.

* Ener-G Egg Replacer: Combine $1\frac{1}{4}$ teaspoons of the powder with 2 tablespoons water and stir well to dissolve.

* Flaxseeds: Grind 1 tablespoon flaxseeds to a powder in a blender. Add 3 tablespoon of water and blend until the mixture becomes thick and sticky.

* Pureed Fruit: Combine $\frac{1}{4}$ cup pureed fruit, such as applesauce, bananas, or softened prunes, with $\frac{1}{2}$ teaspoon baking powder.

* Soft Silken Tofu: Mix together $\frac{1}{2}$ cup drained, soft silken tofu and 1 teaspoon baking powder.

Ten-Minute Brownies

PREPARATION TIME: 10 MINUTES
BAKING TIME: ABOUT 25 MINUTES
MAKES 16 BROWNIES

These rich vegan brownies may start a trend among your friends. Vegan chocolate chips, which can be found in most natural food stores, turn this classic confection into a tasty nondairy dessert.

1/4 cup canola oil
1 cup semisweet vegan chocolate chips
1/2 cup unsweetened applesauce
3/4 cup sugar or natural sweetener
1 teaspoon pure vanilla extract
1 cup unbleached all-purpose flour
1 teaspoon baking powder
3/4 cup finely chopped walnuts

Preheat oven to 350°F. Lightly oil a 6 × 9-inch baking pan and set aside.

In a small saucepan over low heat, combine the oil and chocolate chips, stirring occasionally, until melted. Remove from the heat and set aside.

To a large bowl, add the applesauce, sugar, and vanilla. Blend well. Stir in the chocolate mixture. Whip and blend well. Add the flour, baking powder, and walnuts, and mix just to combine. Spoon the batter into the baking pan. Bake for 25 to 30 minutes, or until the top springs back when lightly touched. Be careful not to overbake the brownies or they will be dry. Let cool completely before cutting into squares. Store in a covered, airtight container in the refrigerator. They'll last for about a week.

NOTE: If you prefer cakelike brownies, use half the amount of chocolate chips.

Mom's Apple Crisp

PREPARATION TIME: 25 MINUTES
BAKING TIME: 35 MINUTES
MAKES 4 TO 6 SERVINGS

Any apple suitable for making pies works in this recipe, including Jonagold, Granny Smith, or Gala. You can use a mix of several kinds of apples, and toss in some dried cherries, cranberries, or raisins if you like. Peeling the apples is not necessary, and you need only one bowl for the preparation.

Apple Filling
4 or 5 apples *unpeeled*, cored, and thinly sliced
1/4 cup raisins
1 teaspoon ground cinnamon
1/4 teaspoon ground nutmeg
1 tablespoon pure maple syrup
1 teaspoon fresh lemon juice
1 teaspoon lemon zest, minced*
1/8 teaspoon salt
1/4 cup orange juice, apple juice, or water

Topping
3/4 cup toasted and chopped walnuts**
1/2 cup rolled oats
1/3 cup unbleached white flour
1/3 cup brown sugar or natural sweetener
1/8 teaspoon salt
3 tablespoons canola oil
2 tablespoons water

Preheat the oven to 400°F.

In a large bowl, combine the apples, raisins, cinnamon, nutmeg, maple syrup, lemon juice, lemon zest, and salt; stir to coat.

(continued)

Desserts and Drinks 207

Pour the juice or water into a 1 1/2-quart baking dish to just cover the bottom, about 1/4 cup or slightly more if necessary. Transfer the apple mixture to the baking dish.

In the same bowl you used to mix the apples (no need to wash it), toss together the walnuts, rolled oats, flour, sugar, and salt. Drizzle in the oil, stirring to coat the mixture evenly. Add the water and stir briefly.

Carefully spread the oat-nut topping over the apples. Bake, uncovered, for 15 minutes at 400°F., then reduce the heat to 350°F. and bake an additional 20 minutes, or until the apples are tender. Remove from the oven and let it cool for 10 minutes before serving.

*NOTE: Use a vegetable peeler or sharp knife to shave off the zest, the thin bright outer skin of the citrus fruit without the white undercoat, taking care not to peel off the bitter whitish tissue under the rind. If you are uncertain of the source of the fruit (whether it's organic or not), use hot water to remove whatever may have been sprayed on the surface.

**NOTE: Toast the nuts on a dry baking sheet in a preheated 350°F. oven for 5 minutes, or until fragrant and lightly browned. Remove immediately from the pan to stop the cooking process.

Fresh fruit is one of the sweetest and most effortless desserts of all. Bright red strawberries and wedges of fragrant melons will easily satisfy a sweet tooth. When new crops of crisp apples and pears arrive at the supermarket in the fall, they're hard to beat. Pomegranates turn up in November, and eating one can keep you busy for a long time. In the winter, tropical fruits such as mango, papaya, and pineapple are full of flavor. Ripe, outstandingly soft persimmons are also heavenly.

Dark Chocolate Rice Pudding

PREPARATION TIME: 15 MINUTES

MAKES 2 SERVINGS

When you feel the need for the intense taste of chocolate, this dessert will satisfy your craving. It's also a great way to use extra cooked rice.

1/4 cup unsweetened cocoa powder
1/4 cup sugar or natural sweetener
3/4 cup soy milk
1/2 teaspoon pure vanilla extract
3/4 cup cooked sweet brown rice or short-grain brown rice*

In a 1-quart saucepan, combine the cocoa powder and sugar. Stir in 1/4 cup of the soy milk to make a smooth, pudding-like mixture. Stir in the vanilla and the remaining 1/2 cup of soy milk. Add the cooked rice and stir to combine.

Bring the mixture to a boil over high heat. Lower the heat and cook, uncovered, at a very gentle boil, stirring frequently to prevent the rice from sticking to the bottom of the pot. Cook for 10 to 12 minutes, until the mixture thickens and you begin to see some rice on the top. The mixture will continue to thicken as it cools.

Remove the pot from the heat, and let the rice rest for a few minutes. Spoon it into serving bowls and eat immediately, or let it cool completely, cover, and refrigerate. It keeps for 2 to 3 days.

*NOTE: Both types of rice work in this recipe; however, sweet brown rice is stickier and better suited to making this dessert.

Coconut Tapioca

PREPARATION TIME: 20 MINUTES
CHILLING TIME: 30 TO 60 MINUTES
MAKES 3 TO 4 SERVINGS

This Thai-inspired pudding is a luscious variation of traditional tapioca. It's wonderful eaten warm or chilled.

- 1/4 cup instant tapioca
- 1 1/2 cups soy milk
- 2 to 3 tablespoons sugar or natural sweetener
- 7 ounces unsweetened light coconut milk*
- 1/2 teaspoon pure vanilla extract

Coconut fat naturally separates from coconut milk in the can. Shake the can well before using. Combine the tapioca, soy milk, sugar, and coconut milk in a saucepan. Let the mixture sit for 15 minutes. This allows the tapioca granules to begin to soften and thicken before you start cooking.

On medium heat, bring the tapioca mixture to a boil, stirring constantly to prevent sticking. Add the vanilla, lower the heat, and simmer for 5 minutes, stirring constantly.

Remove the pan from the heat, and let the mixture sit for 5 minutes to cool. Pour it into individual cups and chill for 1 hour. Serve unadorned or topped with sliced mango, pineapple, bananas, or sweetened strawberries.

*NOTE: Use unsweetened coconut milk free of preservatives. Leftover coconut milk can be refrigerated in a covered container for three days. If frozen, it will keep for six months. (For something extra, you can also blend coconut milk with soy milk and fresh fruit to make a smoothie.)

Quick-Start Blender Tips

If you want a cold drink, using frozen fruit chills the mixture and you won't need to use ice, which dilutes the flavor. If you feed your blender ice cubes, always have it whizzing around at top speed before you add the ice, and add the ice cubes one at a time by dropping them through the opening in the cap.

For light, bubbly juice drinks, add a big splash of sparkling water after you pour the smoothie into the glass. (If you whirl the sparkling water in a blender, the bubbles disappear.)

Keep a stash of very ripe, frozen, unpeeled bananas in your freezer to make blends that resemble soft-serve ice cream. When you want to make a smoothie, remove a banana from the freezer and dip it into a glass of hot water for about 1 minute. As soon as you feel the skin begin to soften, flip the banana over, and dip the opposite end in the water for about 1 minute more. Peel the frozen banana, slice it into 4 to 5 pieces, and it's ready for blending.

Nutrient-Packed Blends

- Using soft silken tofu in your blender creations is a good way to add extra soy to your diet. Tofu is an all-around health food—high in protein and calcium.

- Adding ground flaxseed is a good way to add omega-3 fatty acids.

- Unsulfured blackstrap molasses is an intense, robust sweetener, rich in calcium, iron, and magnesium. Start with 1 teaspoon in blended drinks and taste before adding more.

- Tossing in a small handful of toasted nuts, 2 to 4 tablespoons' worth, is another way to add protein and thicken drinks.

Blueberry Breeze Smoothie

MAKES 2 SERVINGS (ABOUT 2 CUPS)

This smoothie is rich enough to call dessert and nutritious enough for a quick breakfast or late-night pick-me-up.

    1 frozen ripe banana
    1 cup fresh or frozen blueberries
    1 cup soy milk
    $1/8$ to $1/4$ teaspoon pure vanilla extract
    2 tablespoons toasted walnuts*

Dip the banana in a glass of hot water and prepare for blending (see sidebar on page 211). Combine all of the ingredients in a blender, and process until smooth.

*NOTE: Place the nuts in a small, dry skillet over medium heat. Stir the nuts or shake the pan constantly for 3 to 5 minutes, until the nuts are fragrant and lightly browned. Remove the nuts from the skillet immediately to stop the cooking process. Nuts can be toasted ahead of time and will keep in an airtight container for one to two weeks in the refrigerator, or for one to three months in the freezer.

Raspberry Ripple Smoothie

This drink is cool, *crunchy*, and refreshing. Serve it with a cookie on the side.

    1 ripe banana
    ^{1}/$_2$ cup fresh or frozen raspberries
    ^{1}/$_2$ cup orange juice
    4 ounces soft silken tofu, drained

Combine all of the ingredients in a blender and process until smooth.

Pear with Flair Smoothie

Here is a drink full of the flavor of autumn when the new crop of pears and apples are ripening on the trees.

1 pear, peeled, cored, and chopped
½ cup unsweetened apple juice
½ cup soy milk
⅛ teaspoon pure vanilla extract
Pinch of ground cinnamon

Combine all of the ingredients in a blender and process until smooth.

Soporific Tea

PREPARATION TIME: 5 MINUTES
TEA STEEPING TIME: 10 MINUTES
MAKES 1 SERVING

Foods high in tryptophan, such as bananas, chamomile tea, and lettuce, are known for their sleep-inducing properties. When you're ready to relax, this drink could be just what you need.

- 1 chamomile tea bag
- $^2/_3$ cup boiling water
- 1 small banana, sliced
- 3 lettuce leaves, sliced or roughly chopped
- 1 teaspoon fresh lemon juice (optional)

Place the tea bag in a cup and cover with the boiling water. Place a saucer on top of the cup, and let steep for 10 minutes. Drain the tea bag.

Add the tea, banana, lettuce, and lemon juice to the blender. Whirl briefly until smooth, scraping the mixture down from the sides of the bowl, if necessary. Serve immediately.

Café Mexicano

Freshly brewed coffee combined with chocolate is a drink worthy of sipping. Try this on a lazy Saturday morning or a cold winter night for a cozy reward.

1 cup soy milk
1 tablespoon unsweetened cocoa powder
1 tablespoon sugar or natural sweetener
$1/4$ cup strong brewed coffee
$1/2$ teaspoon pure vanilla extract

Place all of the ingredients in a blender, and process until smooth.

Vegan Resources

Three Key Web Sites

www.ivu.org	International Vegetarian Union
www.vrg.org	Vegetarian Resource Group
www.vegansociety.com	Vegan Society, UK

More Web Sites

www.earthsave.org	EarthSave International
www.farmusa.org	Farm Animal Reform Movement (FARM)
www.peta-online.org	People for the Ethical Treatment of Animals (PETA)
www.pcrm.org	Physicians Committee for Responsible Medicine (PCRM)

Important Books

Becoming Vegan: The Complete Guide to Adopting a Healthy Plant-Based Diet, Brenda Davis, R.D., and Vesanto Melina, M.S., R.D., Summertown, TN: The Book Publishing Company, 2000.

Diet for a New America, John Robbins. Tiburon, CA: H. J. Kramer, 1998.

Fast Food Nation: The Dark Side of the All-American Meal, Eric Schlosser. New York: Harper Perennial, 2005.

Food for Life, Neal Barnard, M.D. New York: Three Rivers Press, 1994.

Mad Cowboy: Plain Truth from the Cattle Rancher Who Won't Eat Meat, Howard F. Lyman. New York: Touchstone, 2001.

Poisoned Chickens, Poisoned Eggs: An Inside Look at the Modern Poultry Industry, Karen Davis. Summertown, TN: The Book Publishing Company, 1996.

Vegan: The New Ethics of Eating, Erik Marcus. Ithaca, New York: McBooks Press, 2000.

Index